Pen & Pixel Fusion Volume 2

Fabulous Florals

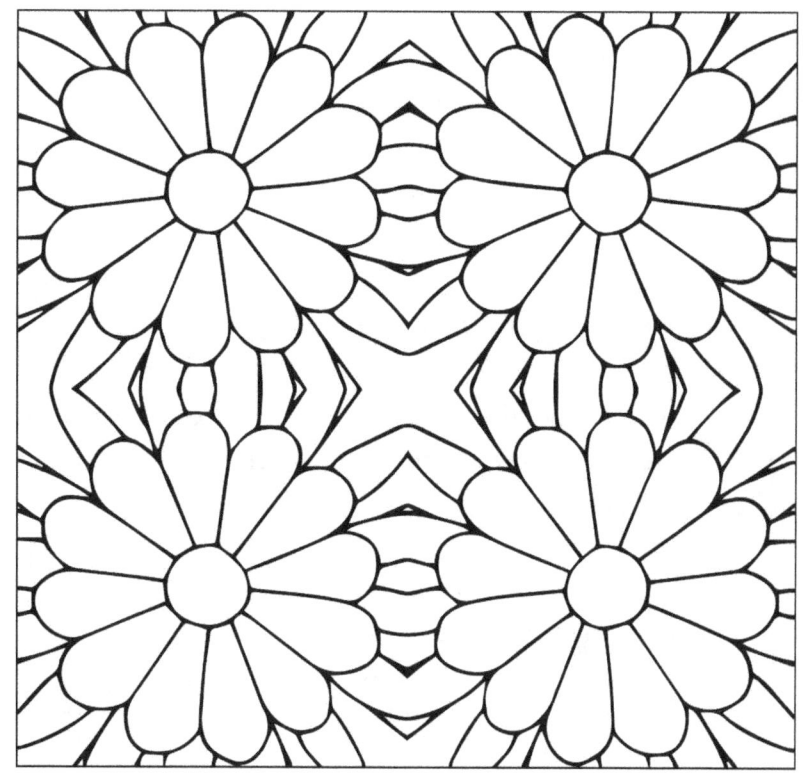

Written and Illustrated by Tina Golden

Cover Art Colored by Kim Vee

Printed in the United States of America

First Printing, 2016

ISBN-10: **1533173184**
ISBN-13: 978-1533173188

Tina Golden
Doodletime Designs
16 Maple Street
Augusta, ME 04330

http://www.DoodletimeDesigns.com

Thank you for purchasing Fabulous Florals, the second volume of the Pen & Pixel Fusion grown-up coloring book series.

There is a running debate among artists and colorists as to which is better, hand-drawn work or digital art. I say, why choose just one? It's the artist's imagination and creativity that makes something art, not the tools they use to do it.

In that spirit, I decided to embrace the wide variety of digital tools available to enhance and transform my original hand-drawn work. The Pen & Pixel Fusion series was born from that embrace and I hope you will love it just as much as I do.

Each book in this series features original designs that have been converted to high quality digital images. You'll see all the weebles, wobbles, and other imperfections that you'll find in hand-drawn art. Each piece of art has then been transformed using various methods to create new designs, such as the symmetrical mandalas and soothing pattern pages included in Fabulous Florals.

With Pen & Pixel Fusion, you get the best of both worlds.

Tips for coloring the images in Fabulous Florals

Let me start by saying there is no wrong way to color. It is supposed to be fun, creative, and relaxing. It's not very relaxing to have negative thoughts or get anxious over how your picture is turning out. Take a deep breath, let go of any negativity, and just be in the moment while you color these designs.

Coloring is a great way to release your inner creativity. A lot of people find that coloring inspires them to be creative in other areas of their lives, so when you're feeling stuck about something – color!

I recommend colored pencils or other dry media with this book, but you can use gel pens or markers if you take some care. Wet media can bleed through the pages onto another design. To avoid that, make sure to put an extra sheet of paper or card-stock behind the page you're coloring. There are three convenient blotter sheets included at the back of the book that you can use for this purpose.

If there is an image that you really want to turn out a certain way, feel free to photocopy the image onto the paper of your choice. I find a light-weight card stock perfect for my own coloring. It holds up nicely to markers and gel pens, but has enough tooth to work great with colored pencils, as well.

Photocopying your favorite designs can really allow you to relax and go with the flow when coloring as it takes all the worry out of it. It's an automatic do-over because you still have the original to print another. It's also a great way to try a different coloring palette.

I enjoy seeing how other people color my designs and learning about their techniques, so I'd love to have you share any finished pieces on my Facebook page or tag me on any social media channels we're both on. And both authors and artists thrive on reviews so please help me out by posting a review on Amazon – your support will enable me to keep bringing you new and exciting coloring books.

See you there!

Tina Golden

Get a free mini coloring book to print when you join the Doodletime Designs Coloring Crew. Members get a new exclusive coloring page monthly, as well as other perks.

Sign up here: http://DoodletimeDesigns.com/free-mini-coloring-book

Connect with me on Facebook for sneak peaks at works-in-progress and other fun stuff.

https://www.facebook.com/DoodletimeOriginals

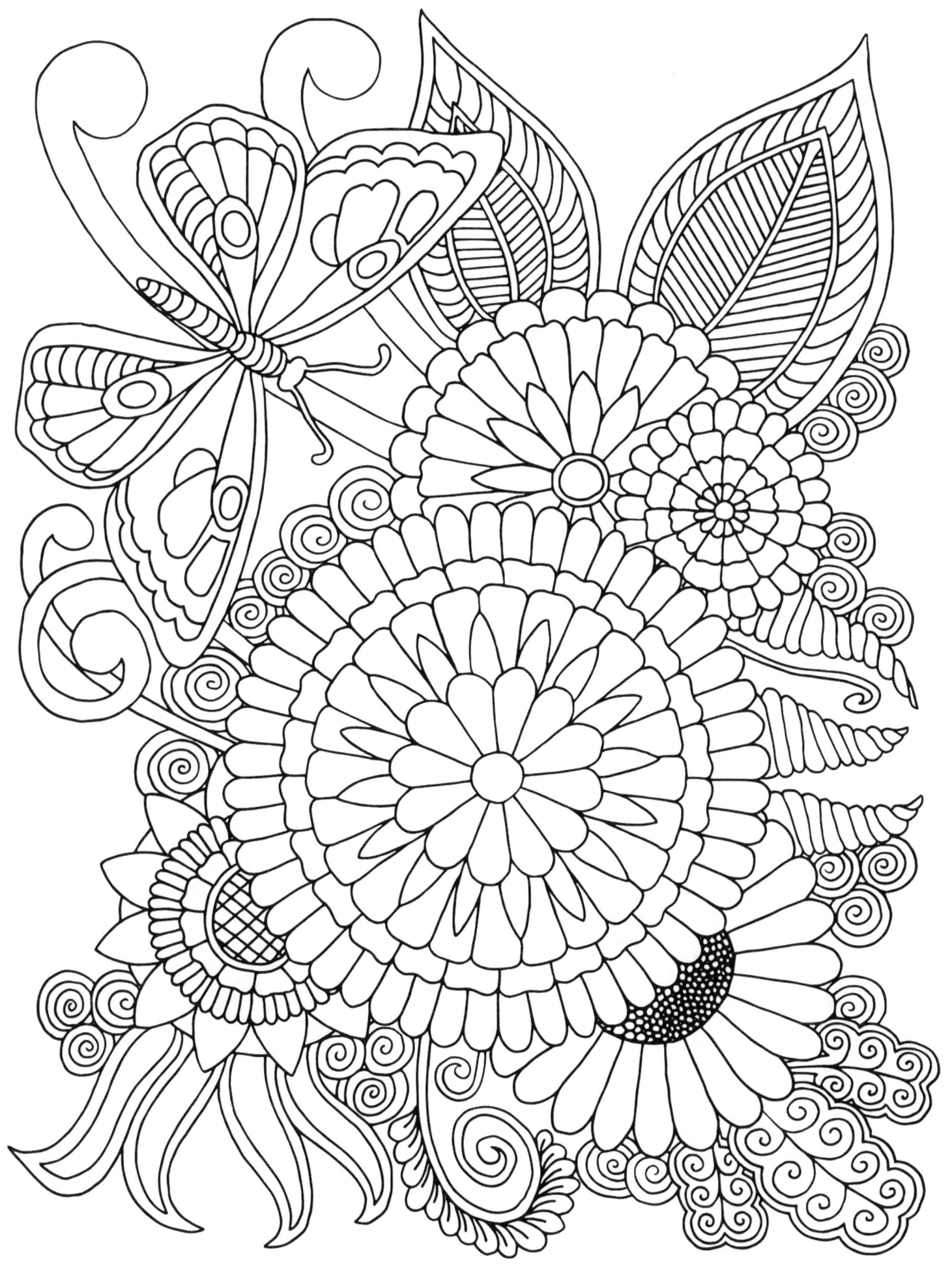

Artist: Tina Golden

Book: Fabulous Florals (Pen & Pixel Fusion Vol. 2)

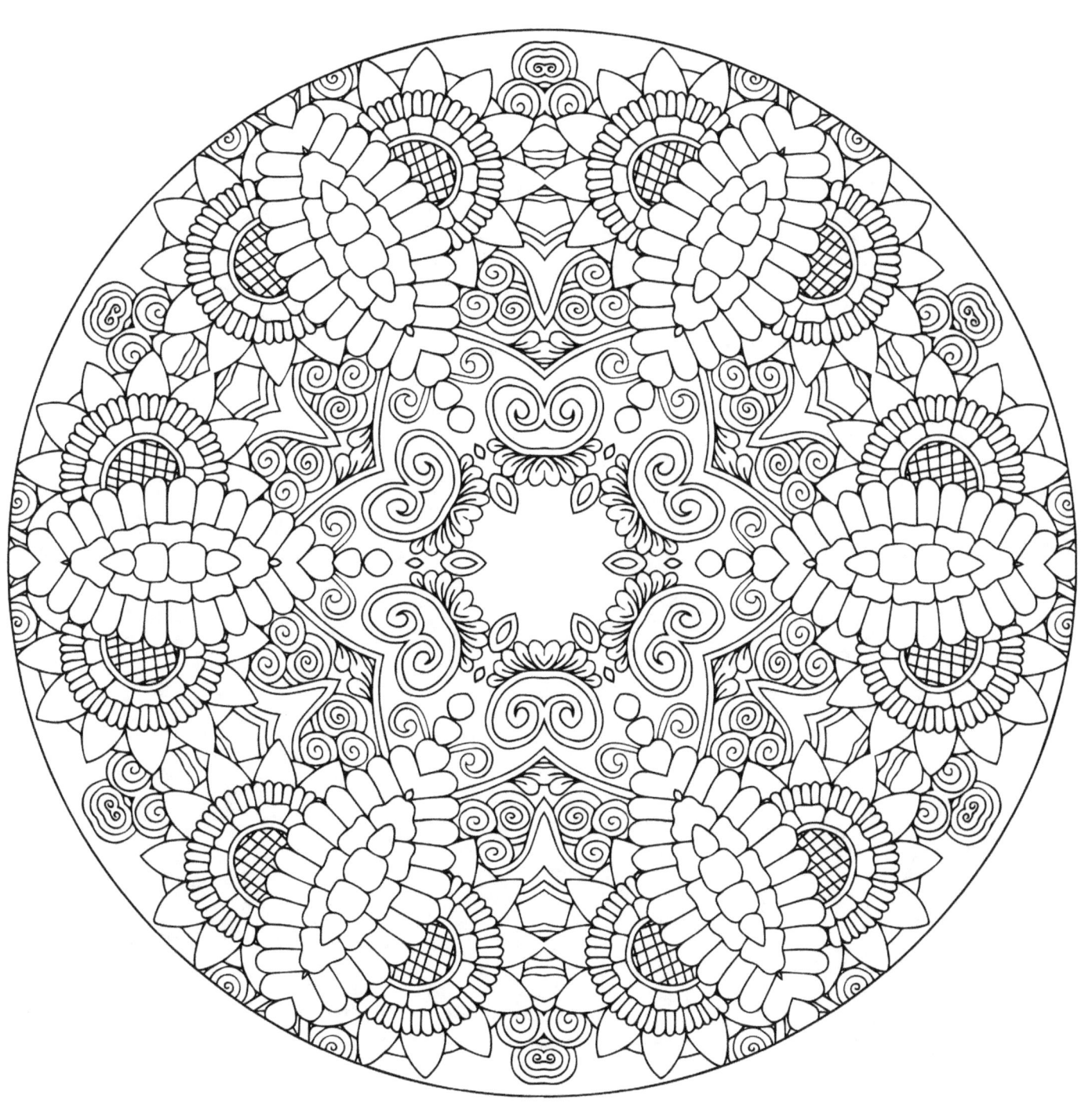

Artist: Tina Golden

Book: Fabulous Florals (Pen & Pixel Fusion Vol. 2)

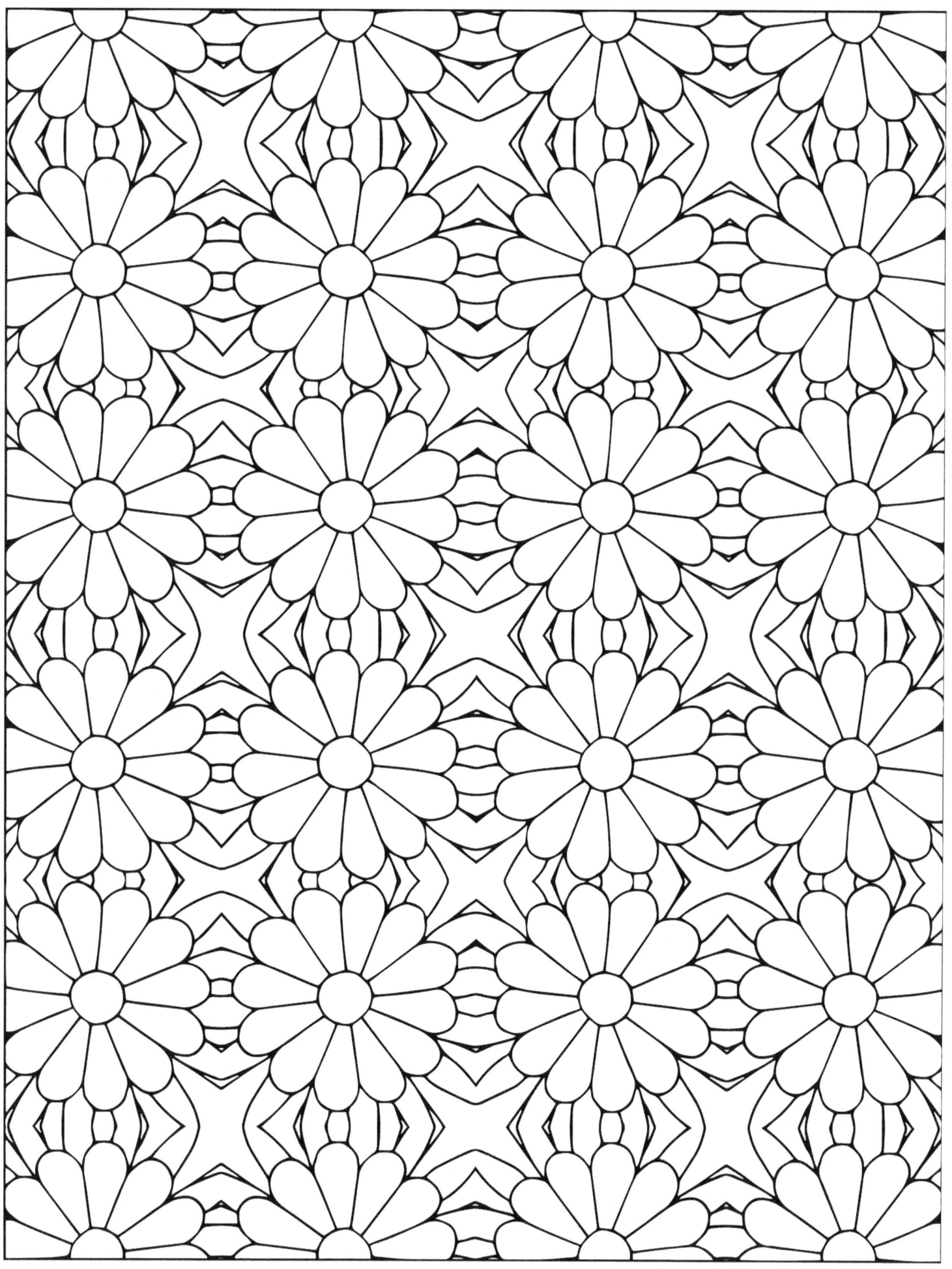

Artist: Tina Golden

Book: Fabulous Florals (Pen & Pixel Fusion Vol. 2)

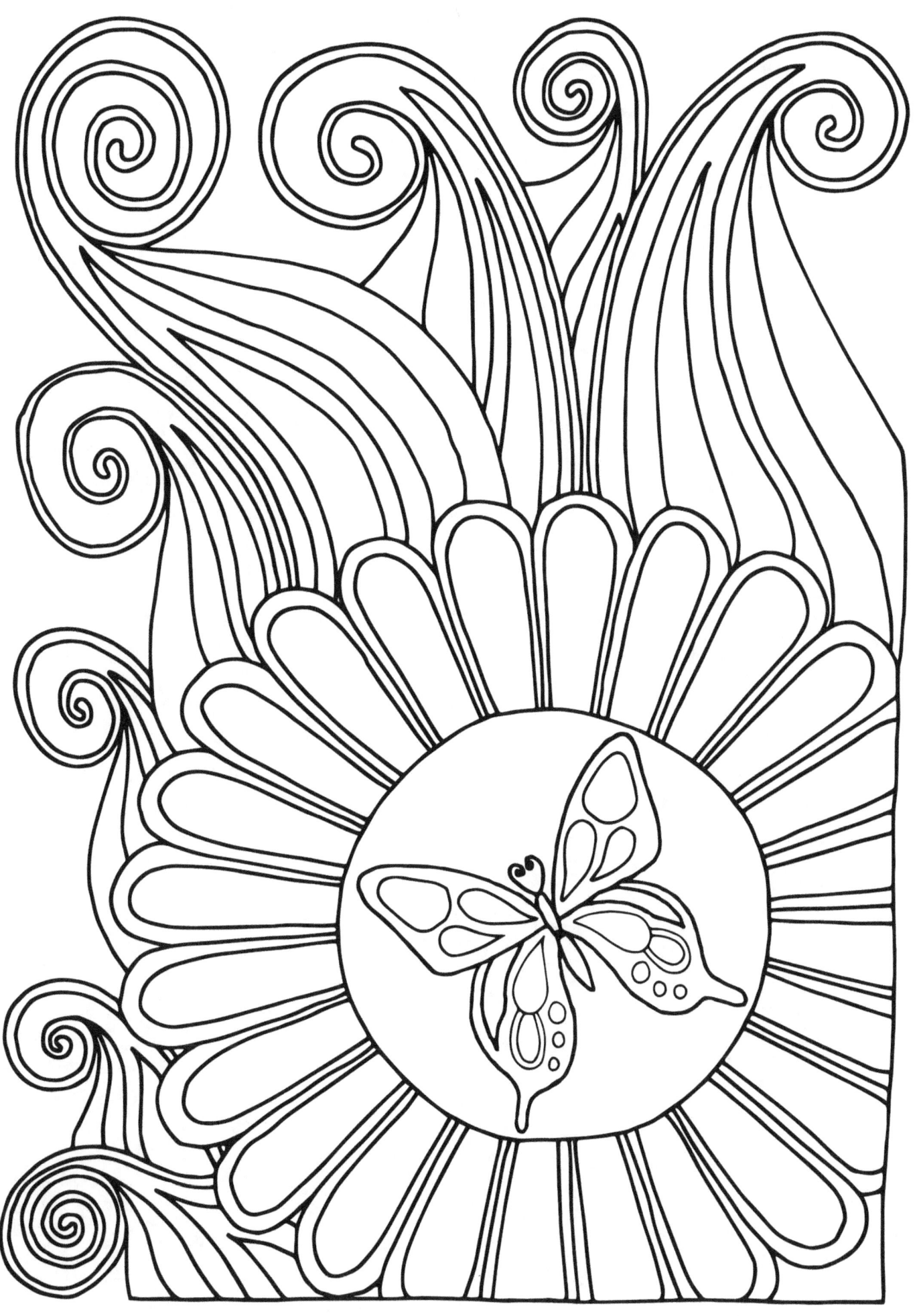

Artist: Tina Golden

Book: Fabulous Florals (Pen & Pixel Fusion Vol. 2)

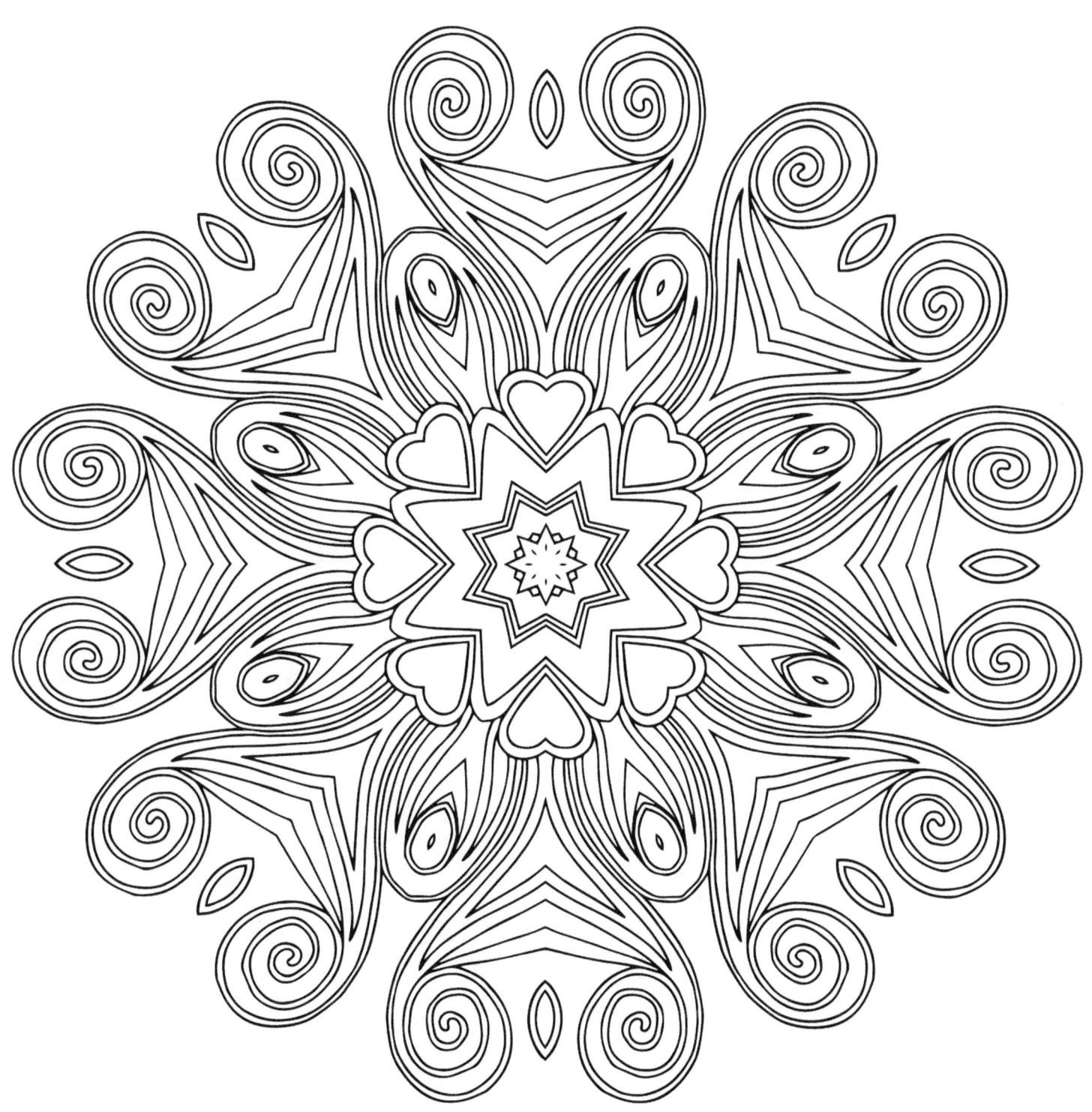

Artist: Tina Golden

Book: Fabulous Florals (Pen & Pixel Fusion Vol. 2)

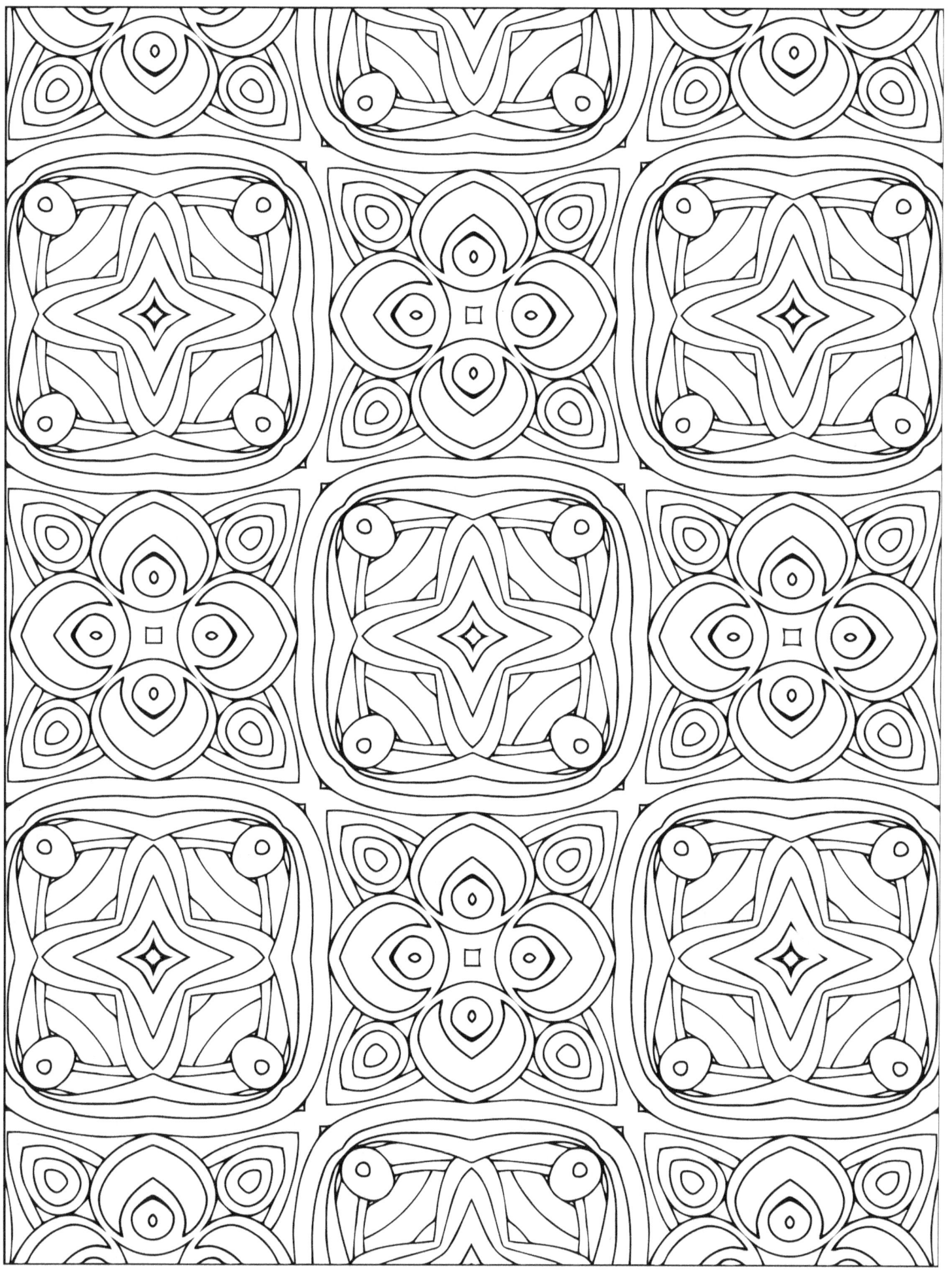

Artist: Tina Golden

Book: Fabulous Florals (Pen & Pixel Fusion Vol. 2)

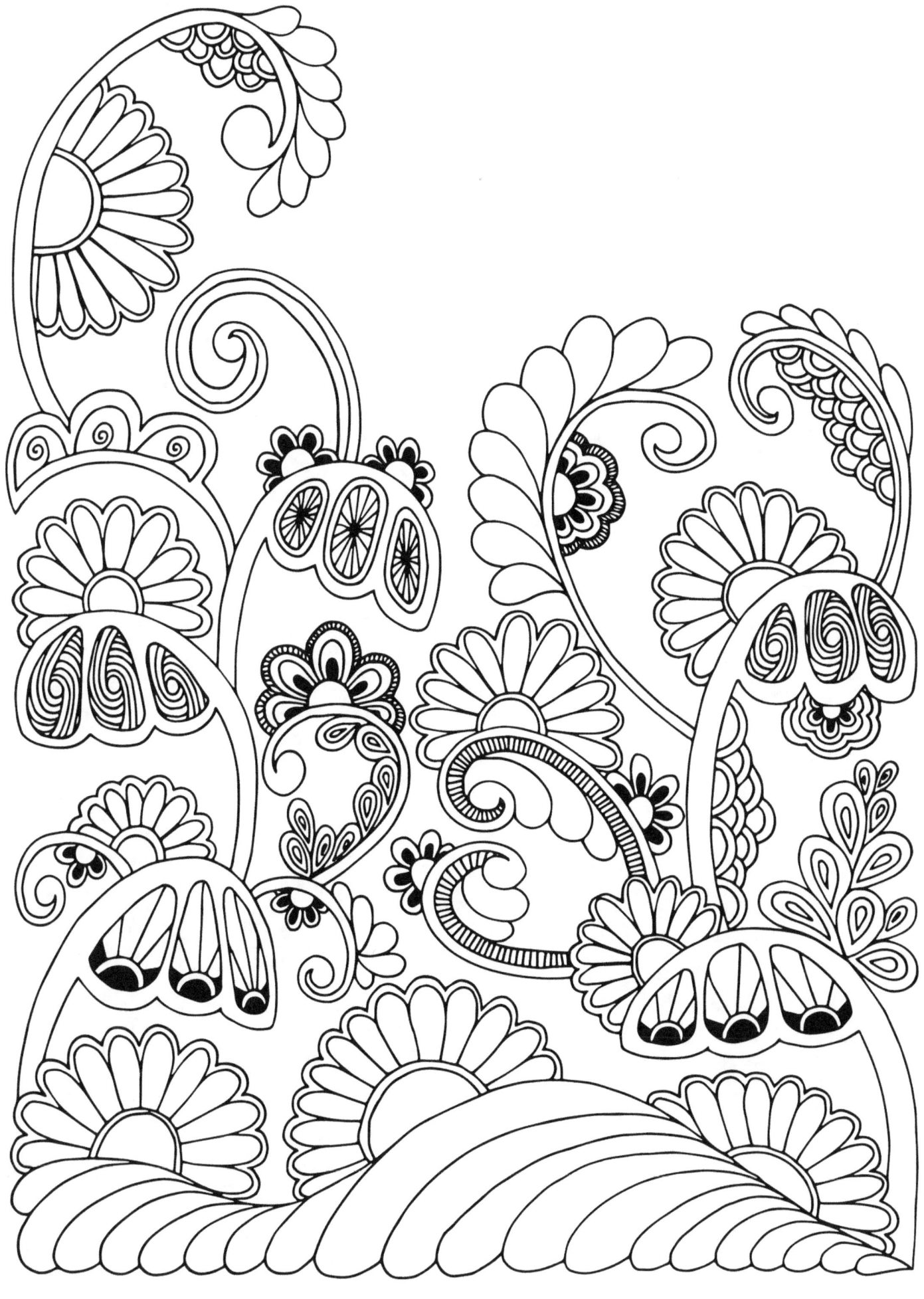

Artist: Tina Golden

Book: Fabulous Florals (Pen & Pixel Fusion Vol. 2)

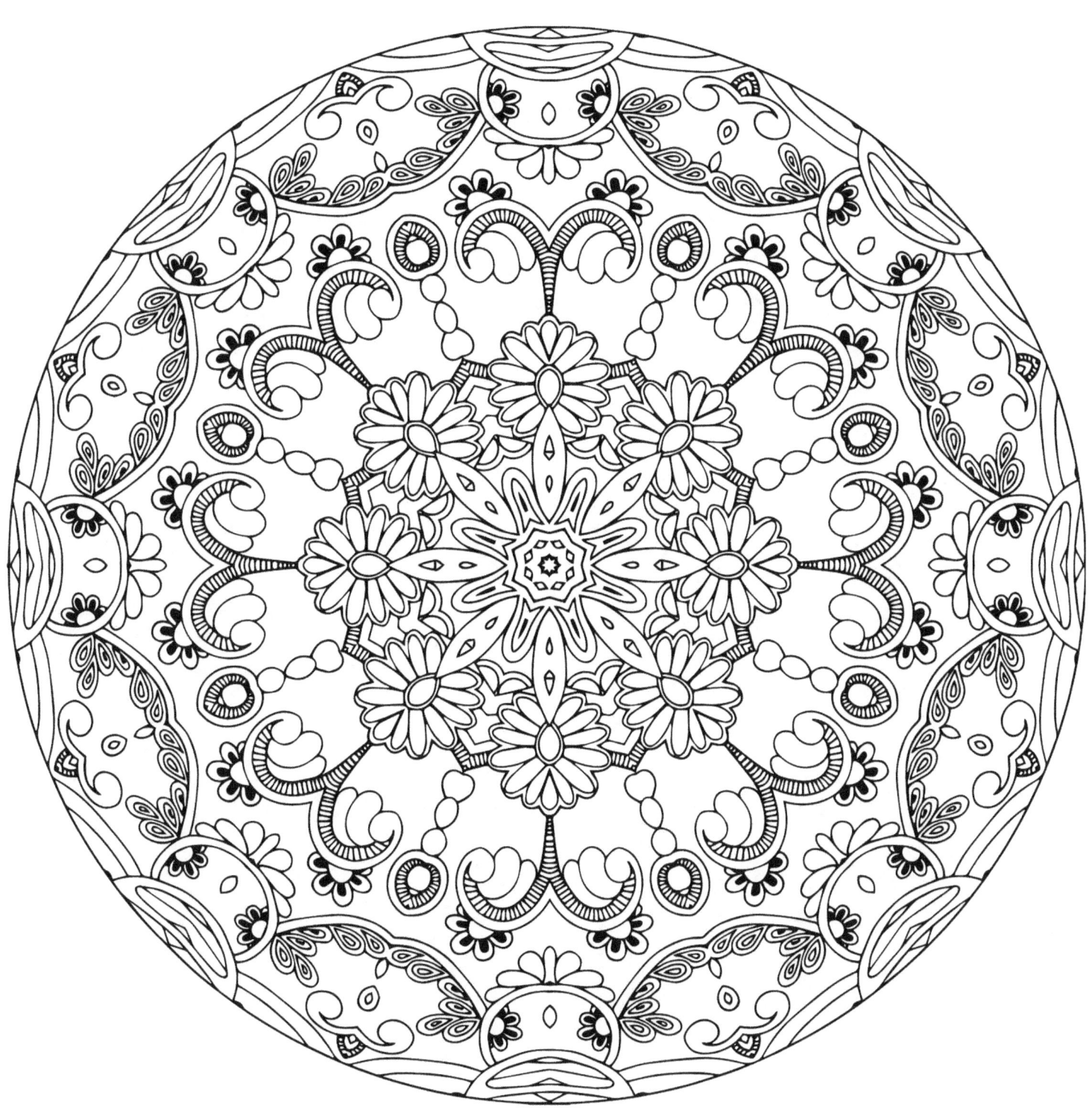

Artist: Tina Golden

Book: Fabulous Florals (Pen & Pixel Fusion Vol. 2)

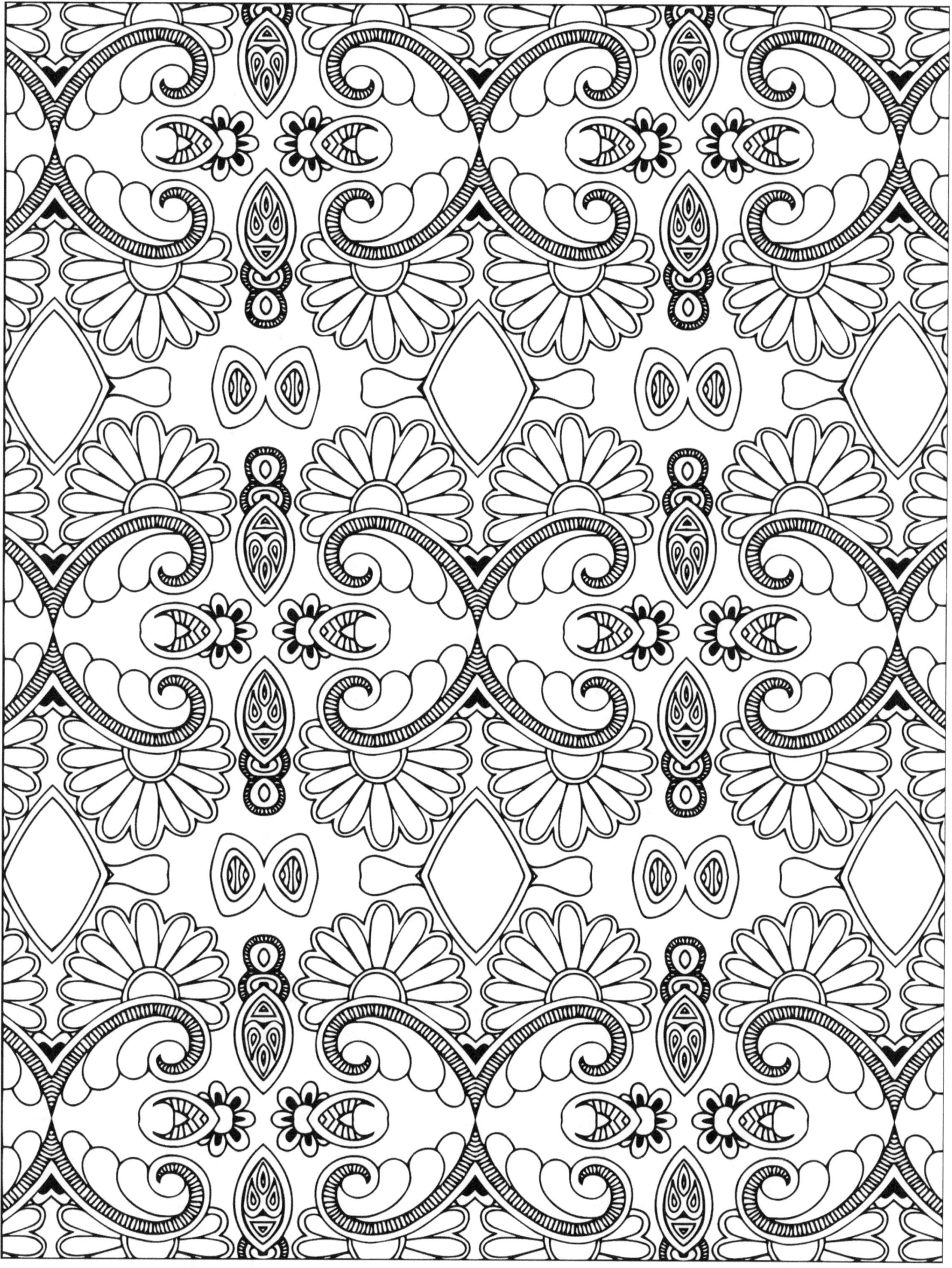

Artist: Tina Golden

Book: Fabulous Florals (Pen & Pixel Fusion Vol. 2)

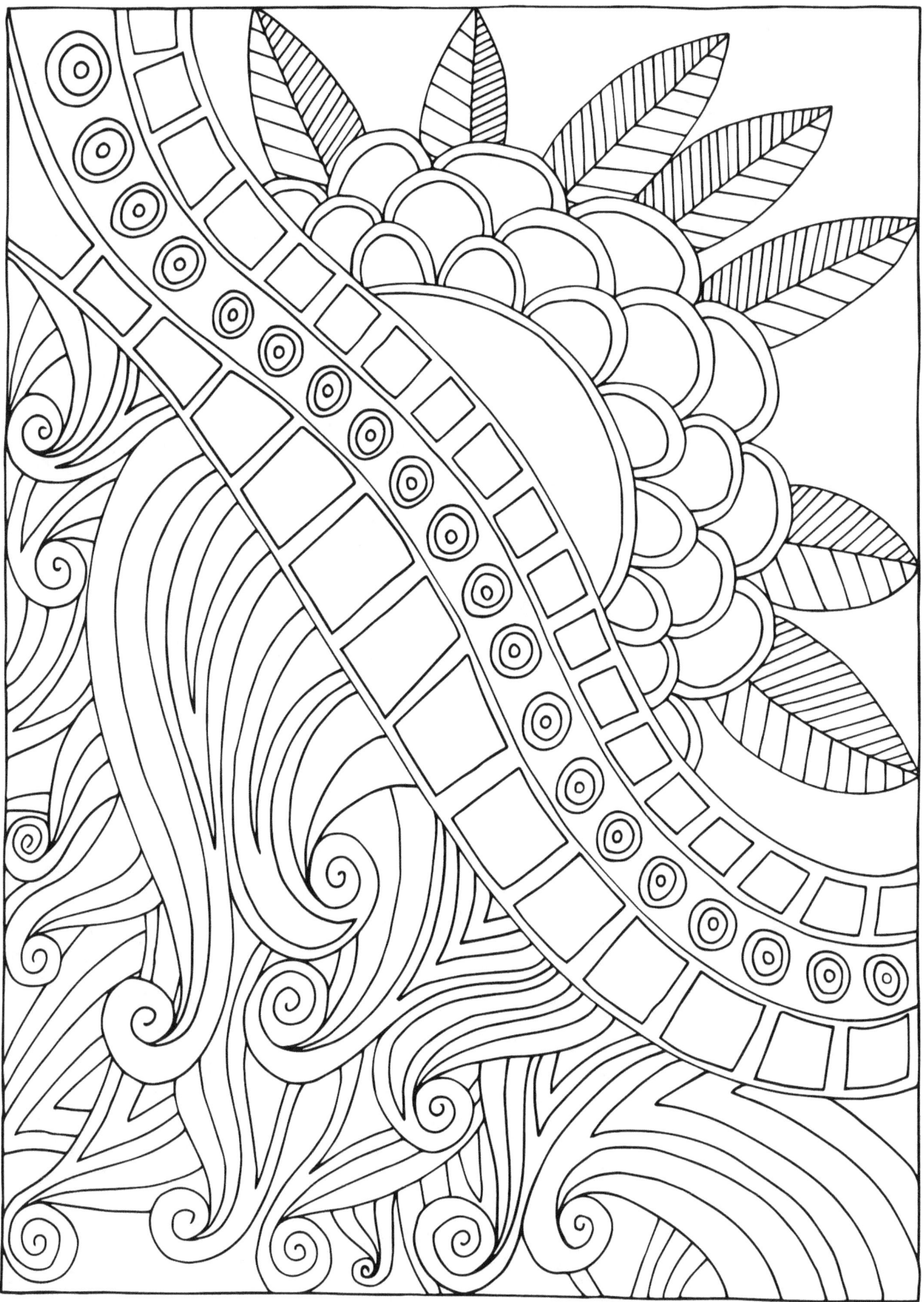

Artist: Tina Golden

Book: Fabulous Florals (Pen & Pixel Fusion Vol. 2)

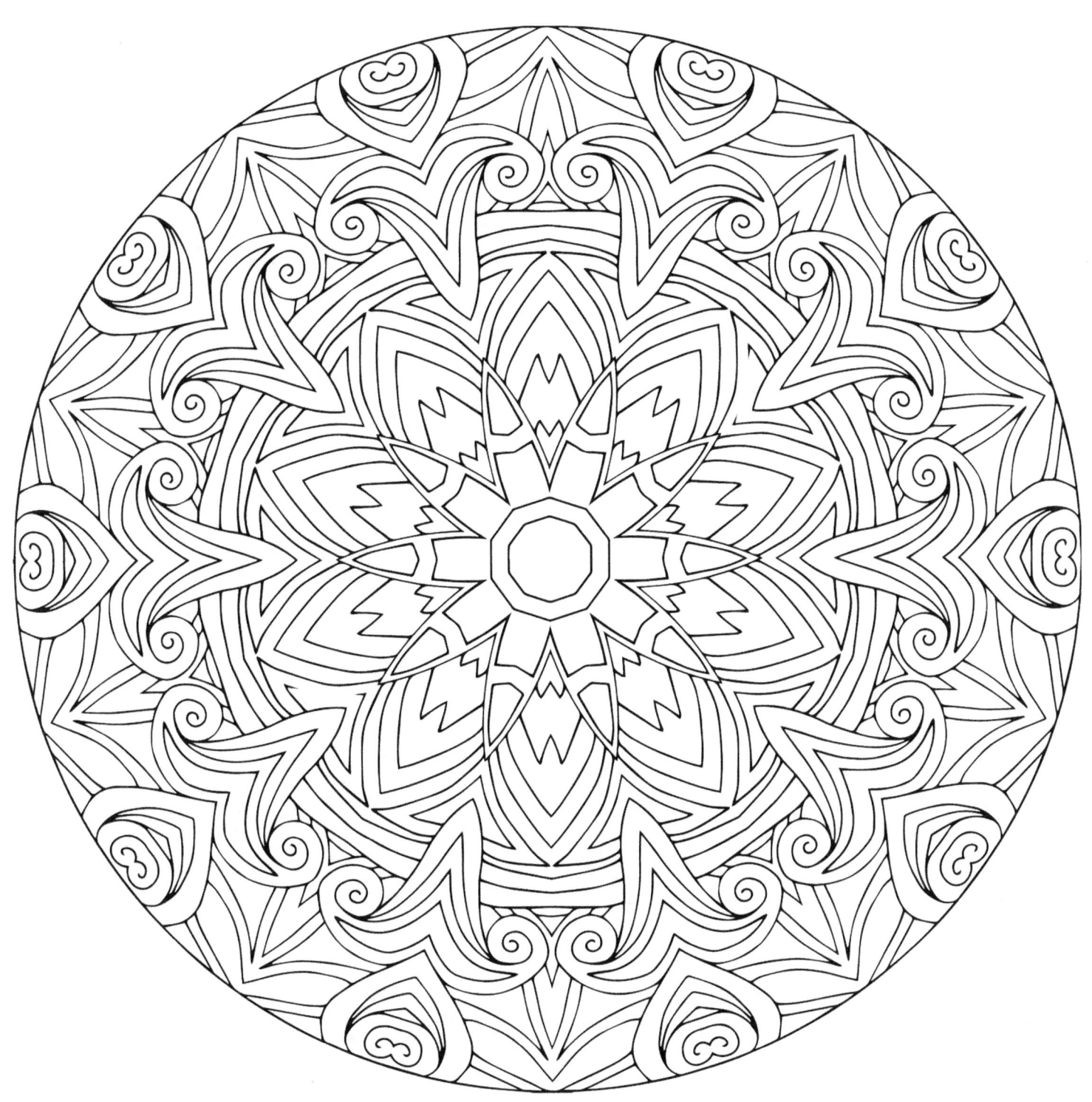

Artist: Tina Golden

Book: Fabulous Florals (Pen & Pixel Fusion Vol. 2)

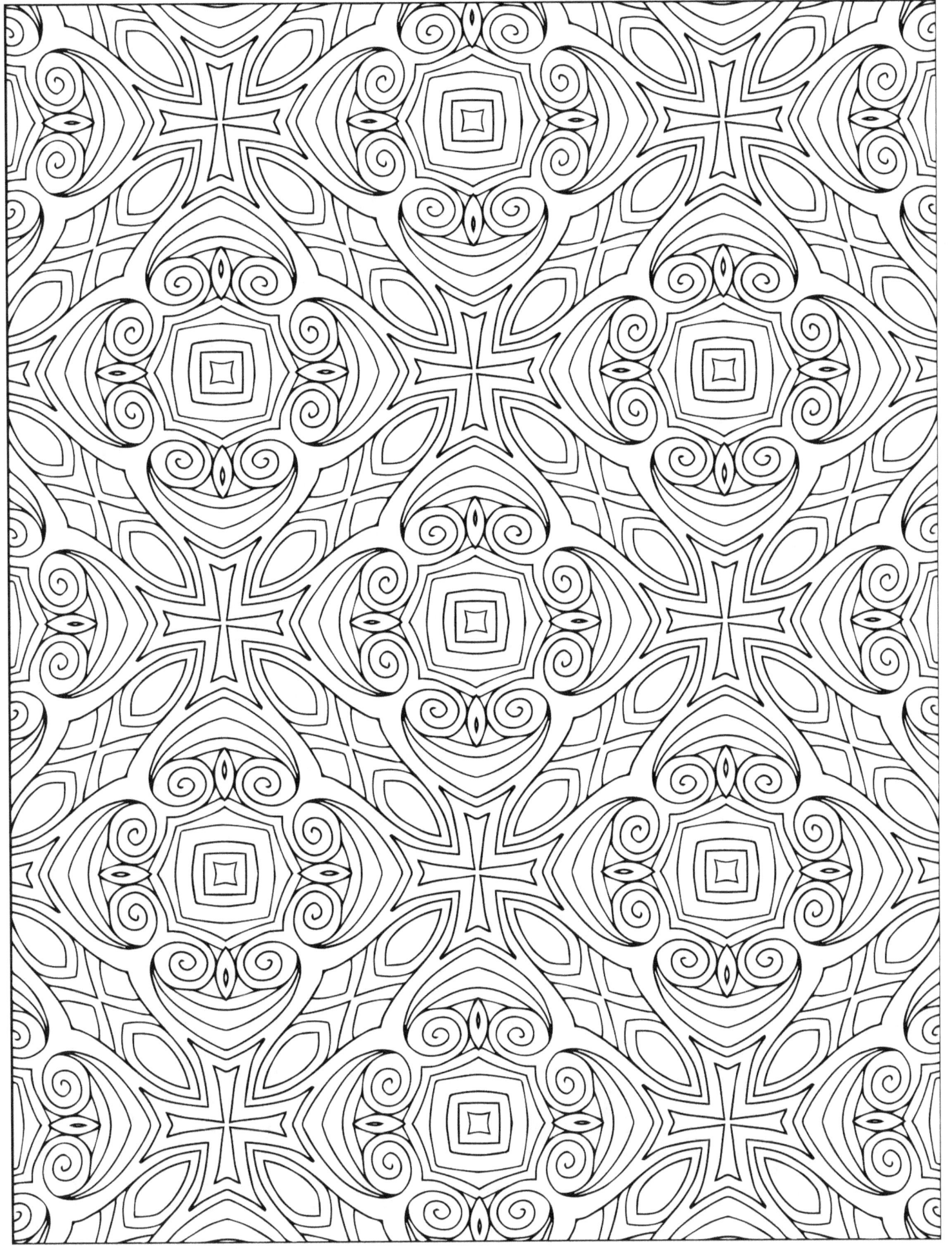

Artist: Tina Golden

Book: Fabulous Florals (Pen & Pixel Fusion Vol. 2)

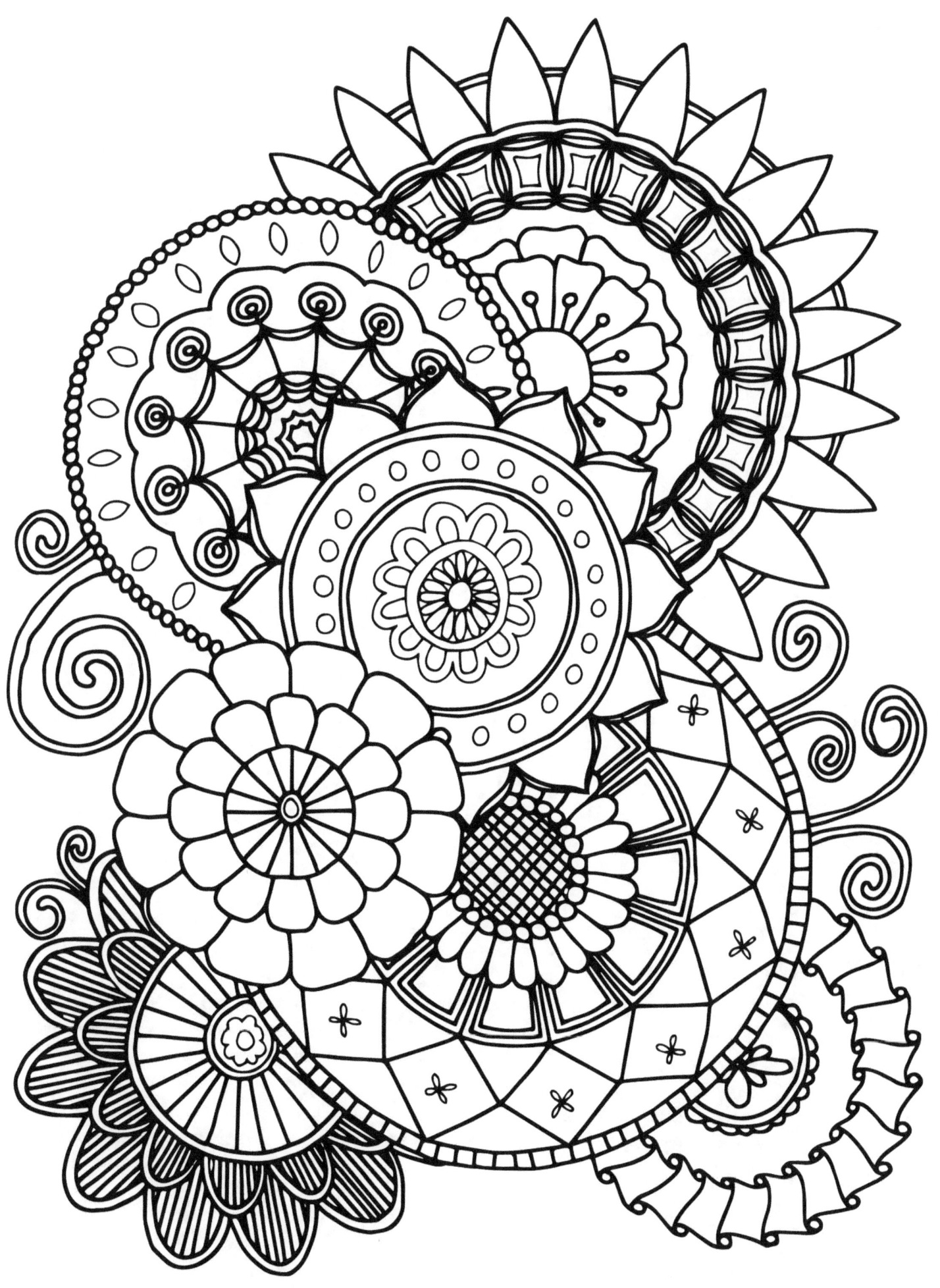

Artist: Tina Golden

Book: Fabulous Florals (Pen & Pixel Fusion Vol. 2)

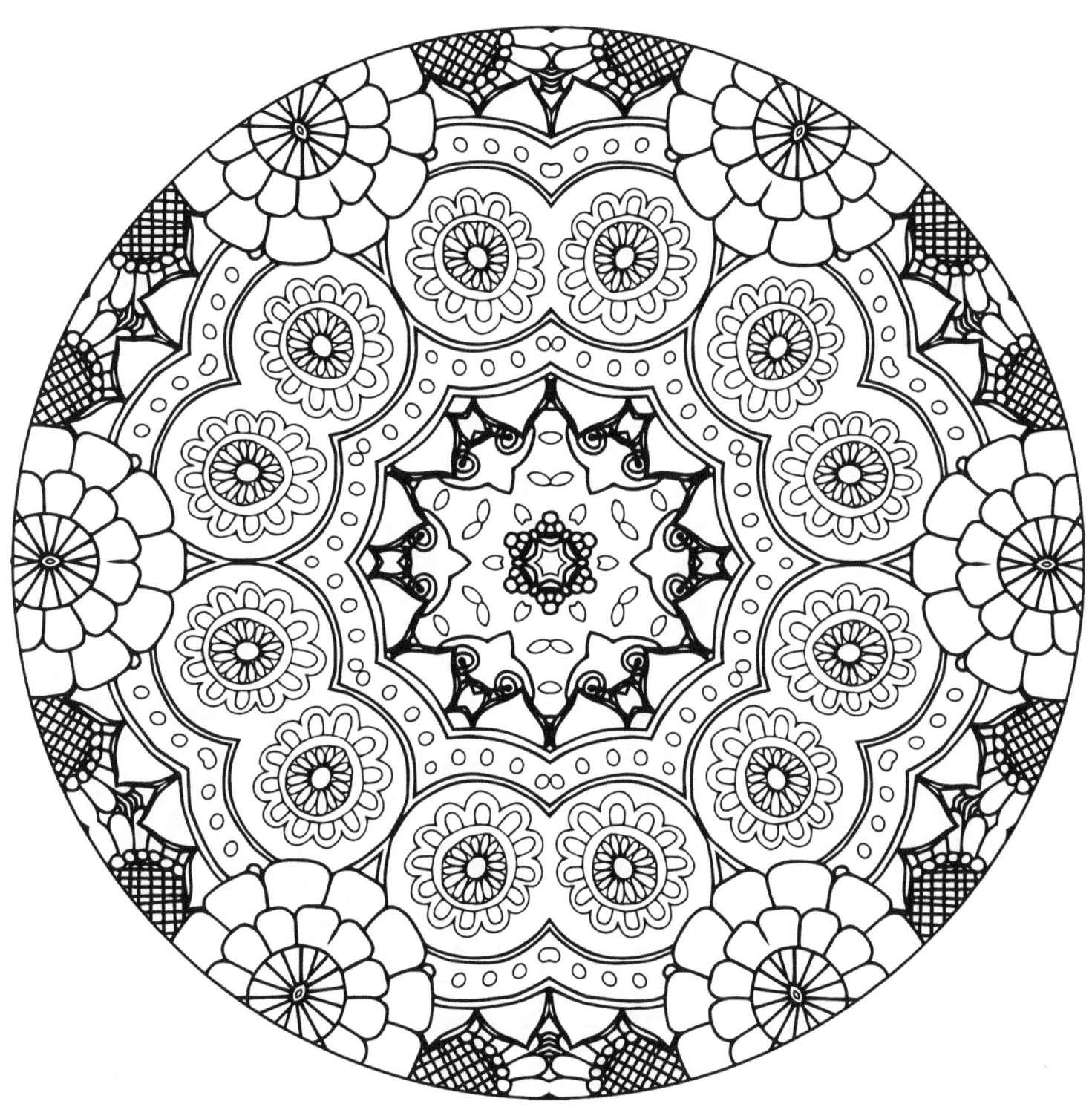

Artist: Tina Golden

Book: Fabulous Florals (Pen & Pixel Fusion Vol. 2)

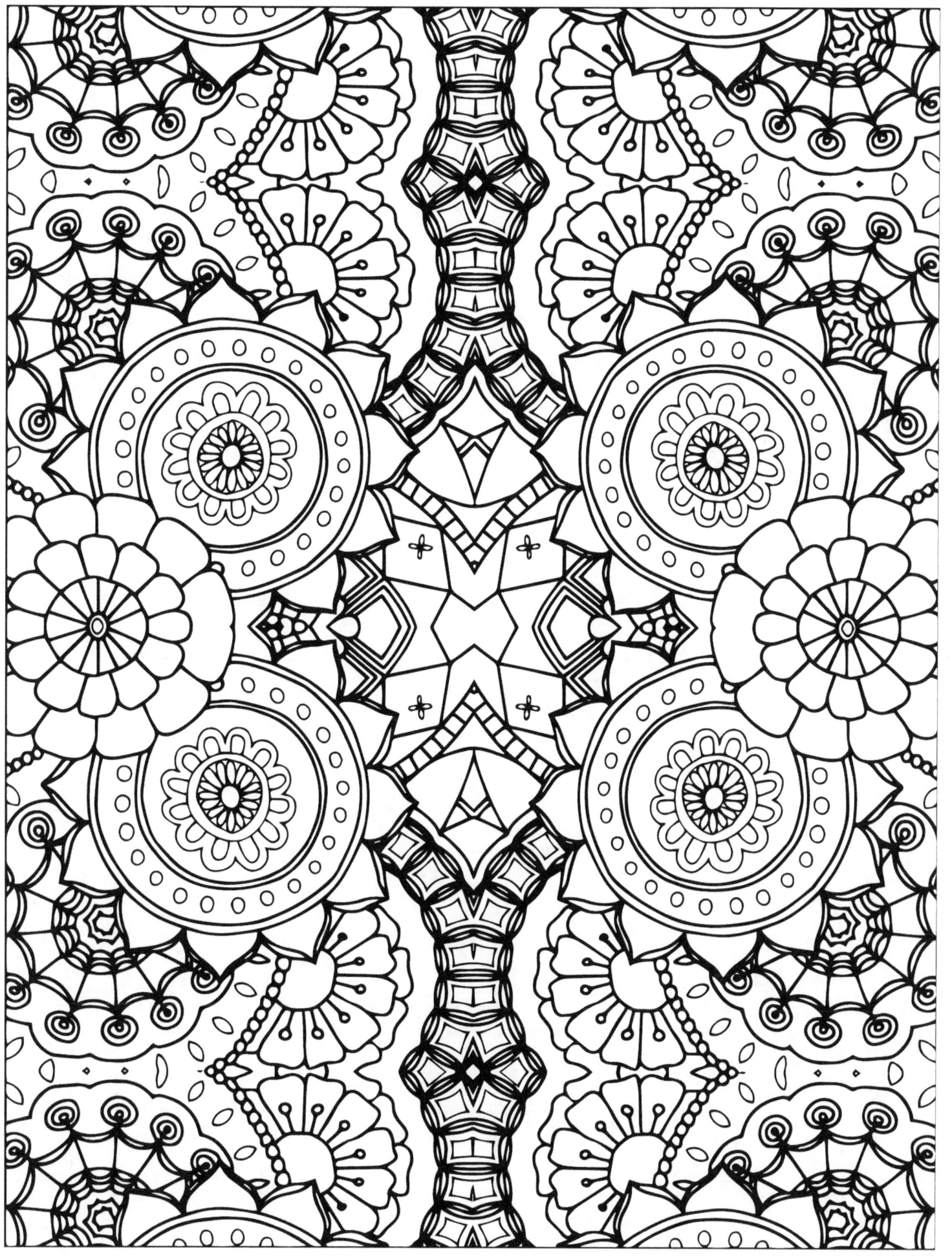

Artist: Tina Golden

Book: Fabulous Florals (Pen & Pixel Fusion Vol. 2)

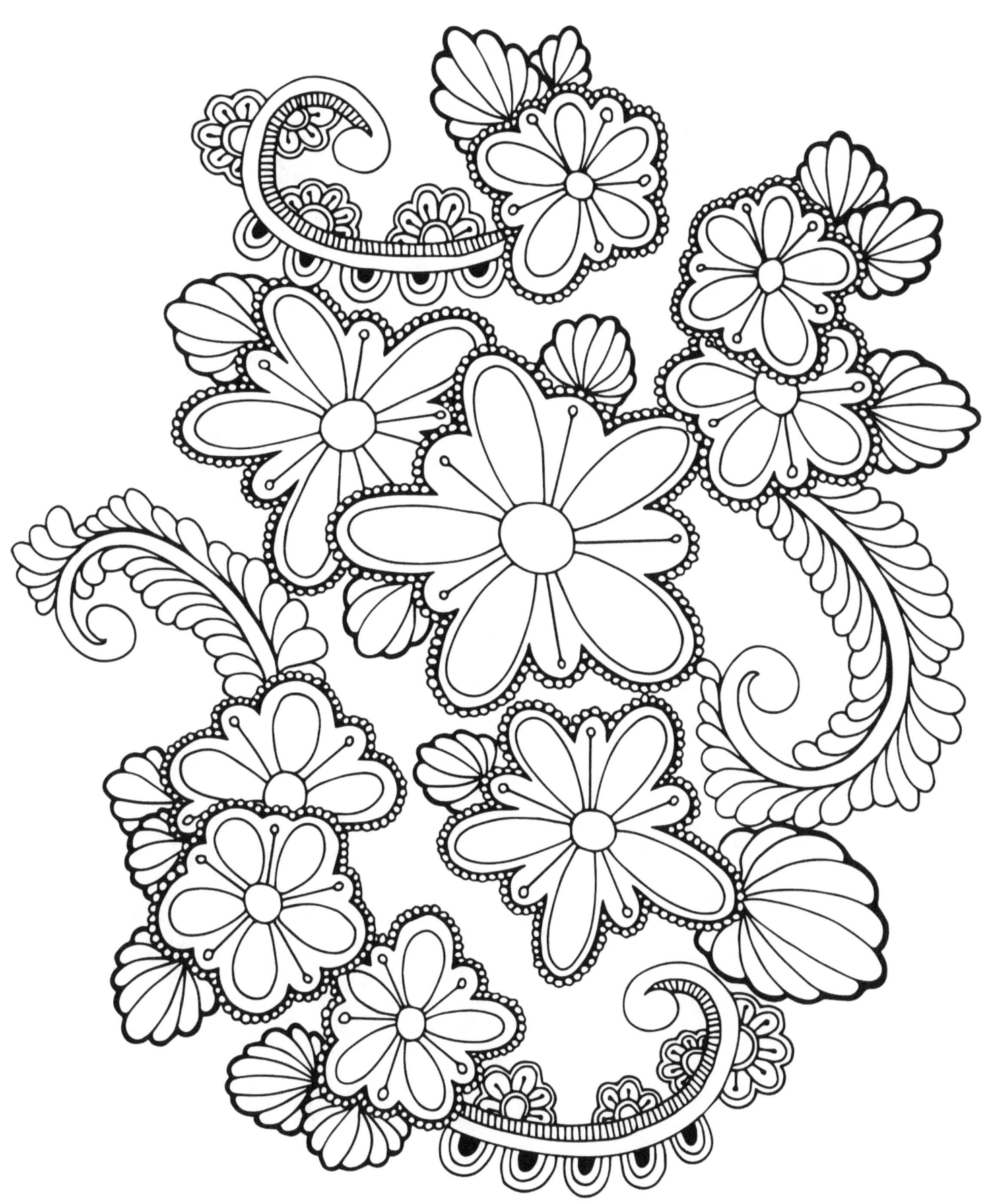

Artist: Tina Golden

Book: Fabulous Florals (Pen & Pixel Fusion Vol. 2)

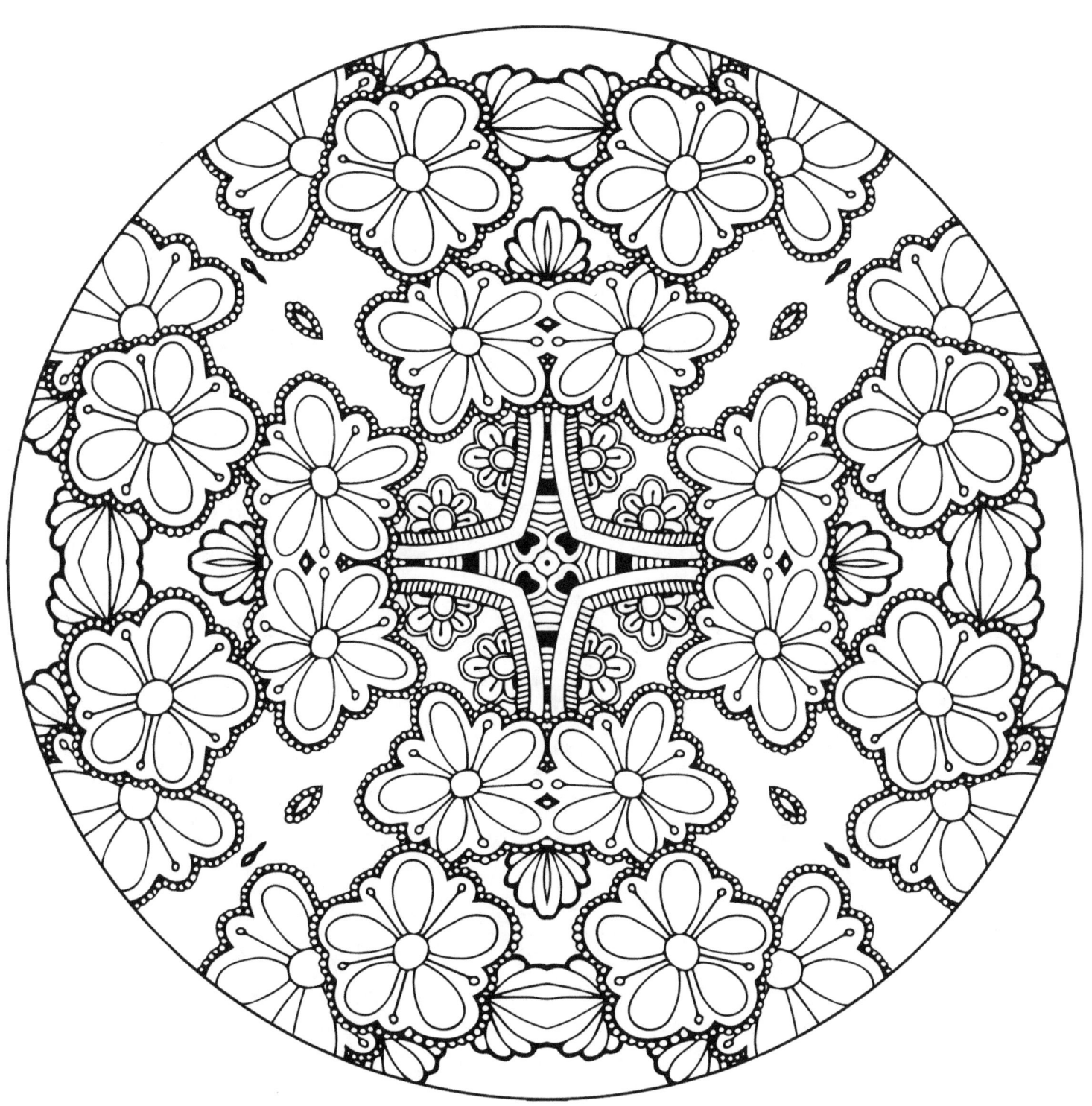

Artist: Tina Golden

Book: Fabulous Florals (Pen & Pixel Fusion Vol. 2)

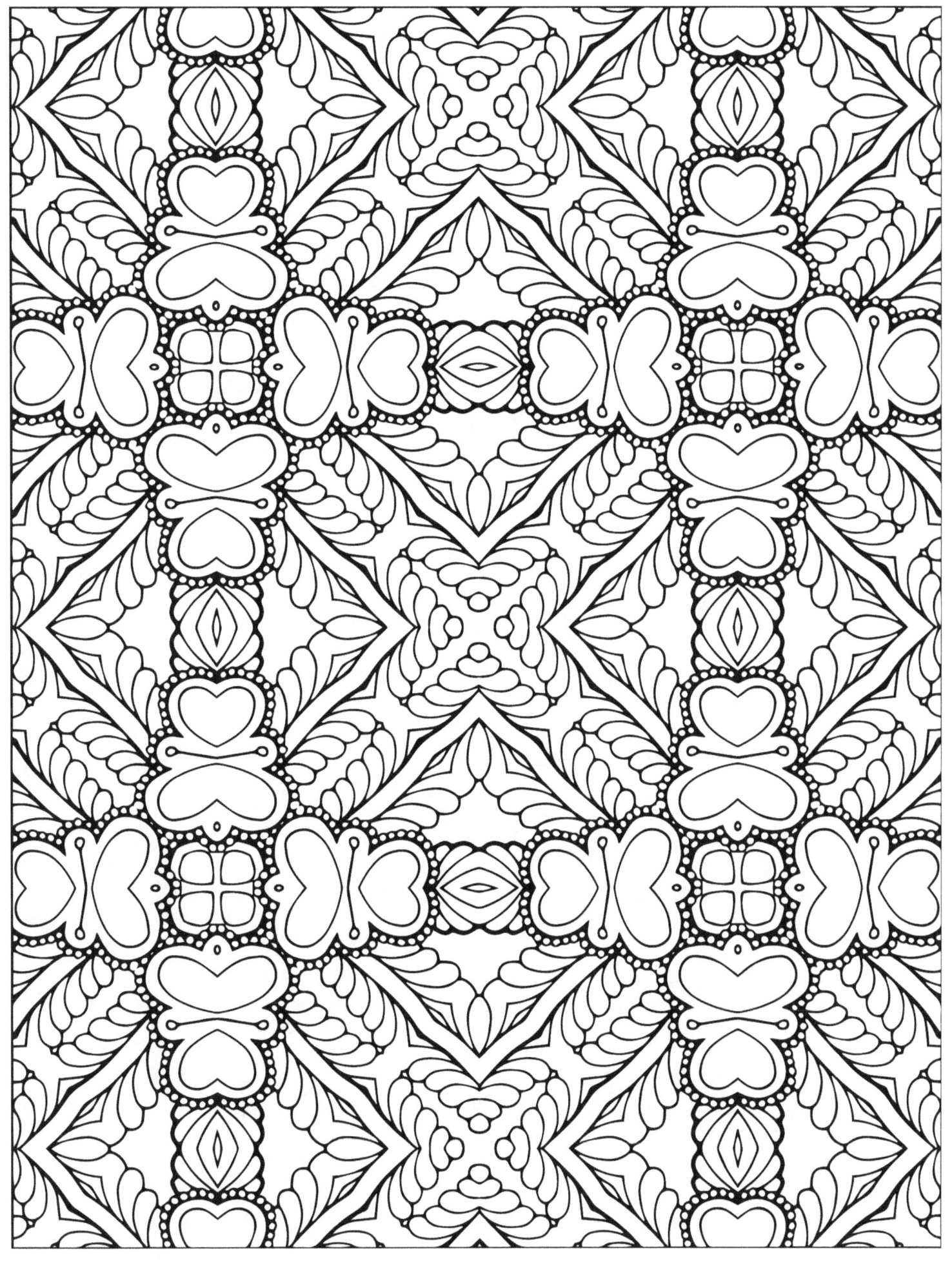

Artist: Tina Golden

Book: Fabulous Florals (Pen & Pixel Fusion Vol. 2)

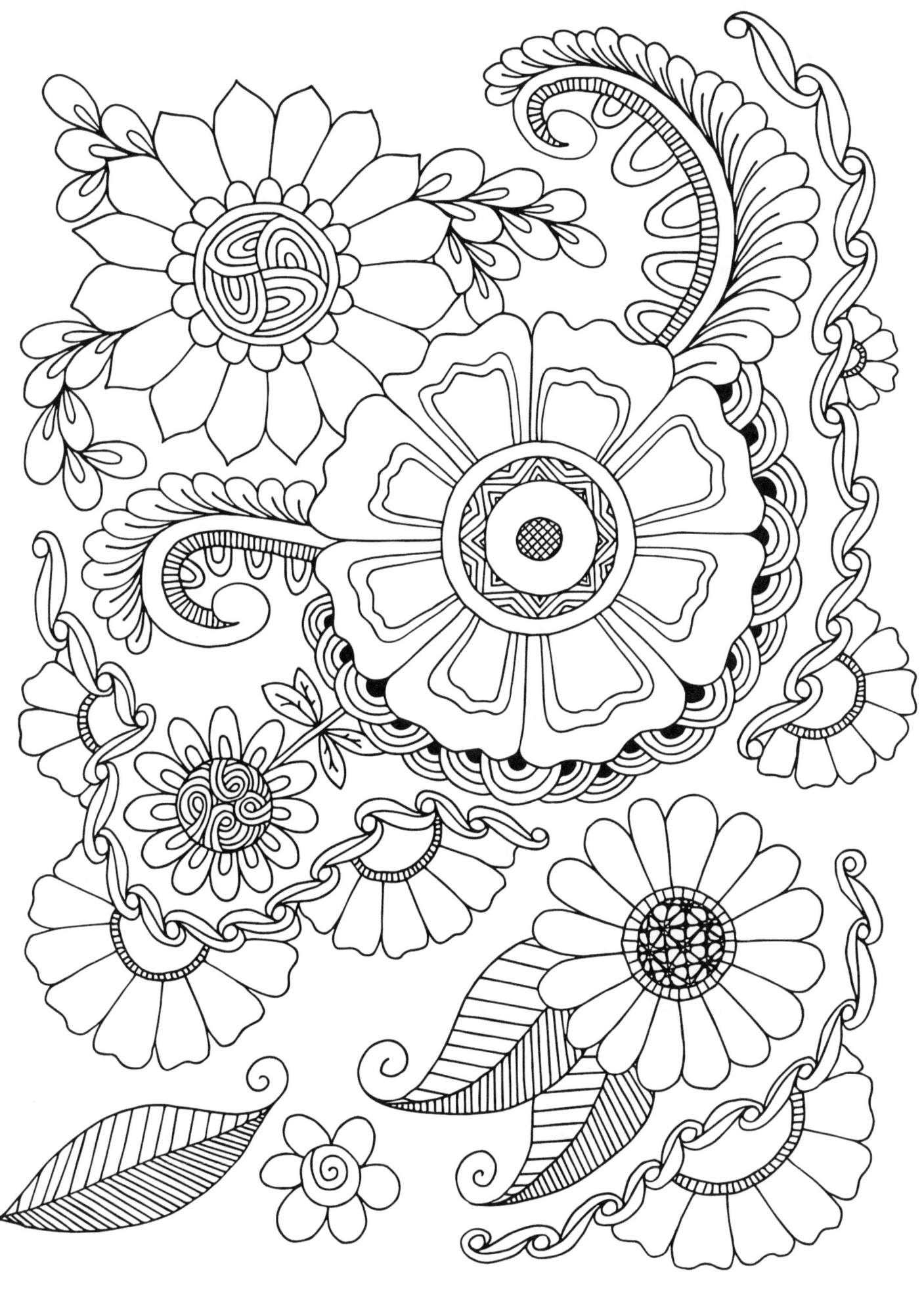

Artist: Tina Golden

Book: Fabulous Florals (Pen & Pixel Fusion Vol. 2)

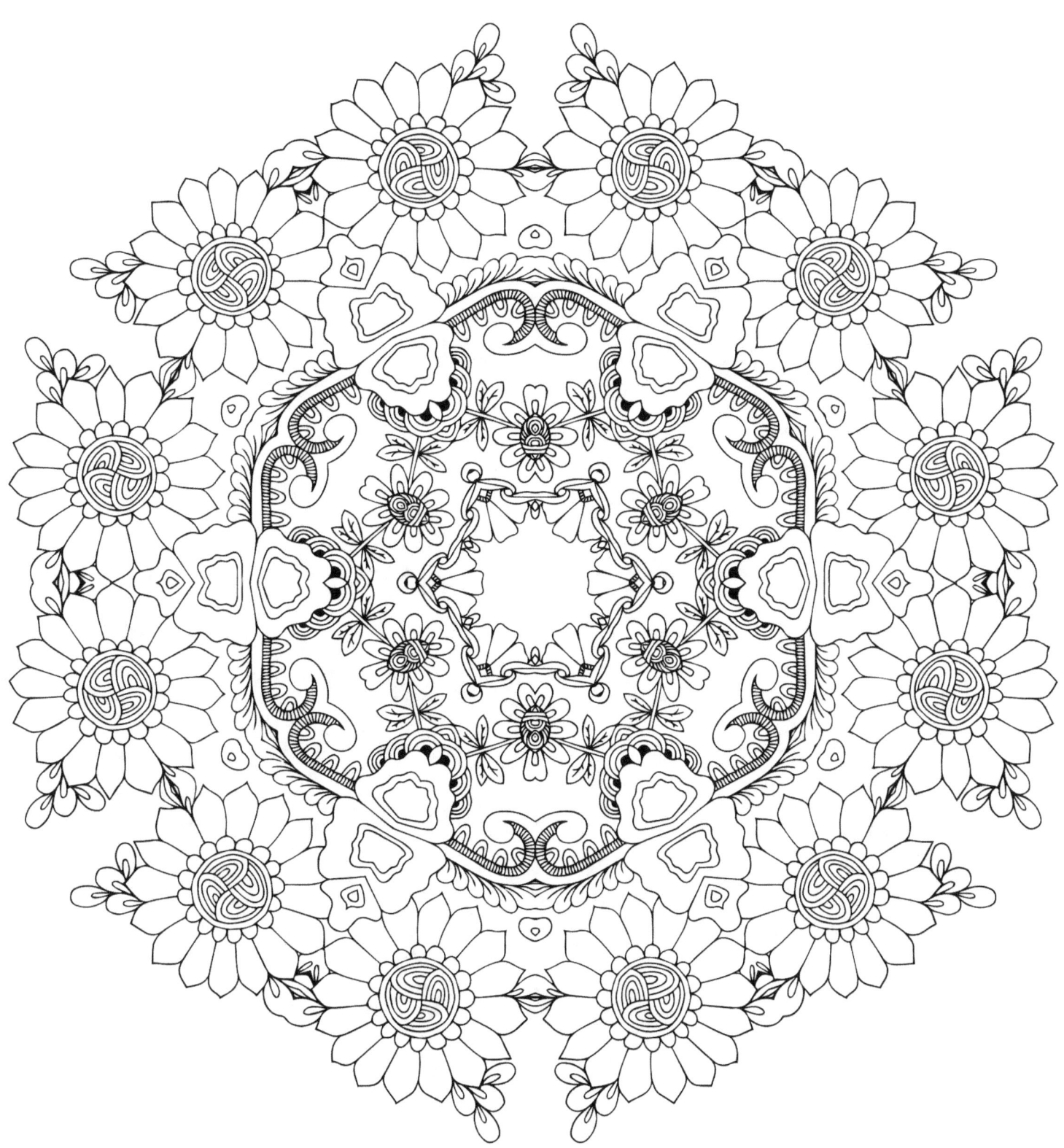

Artist: Tina Golden

Book: Fabulous Florals (Pen & Pixel Fusion Vol. 2)

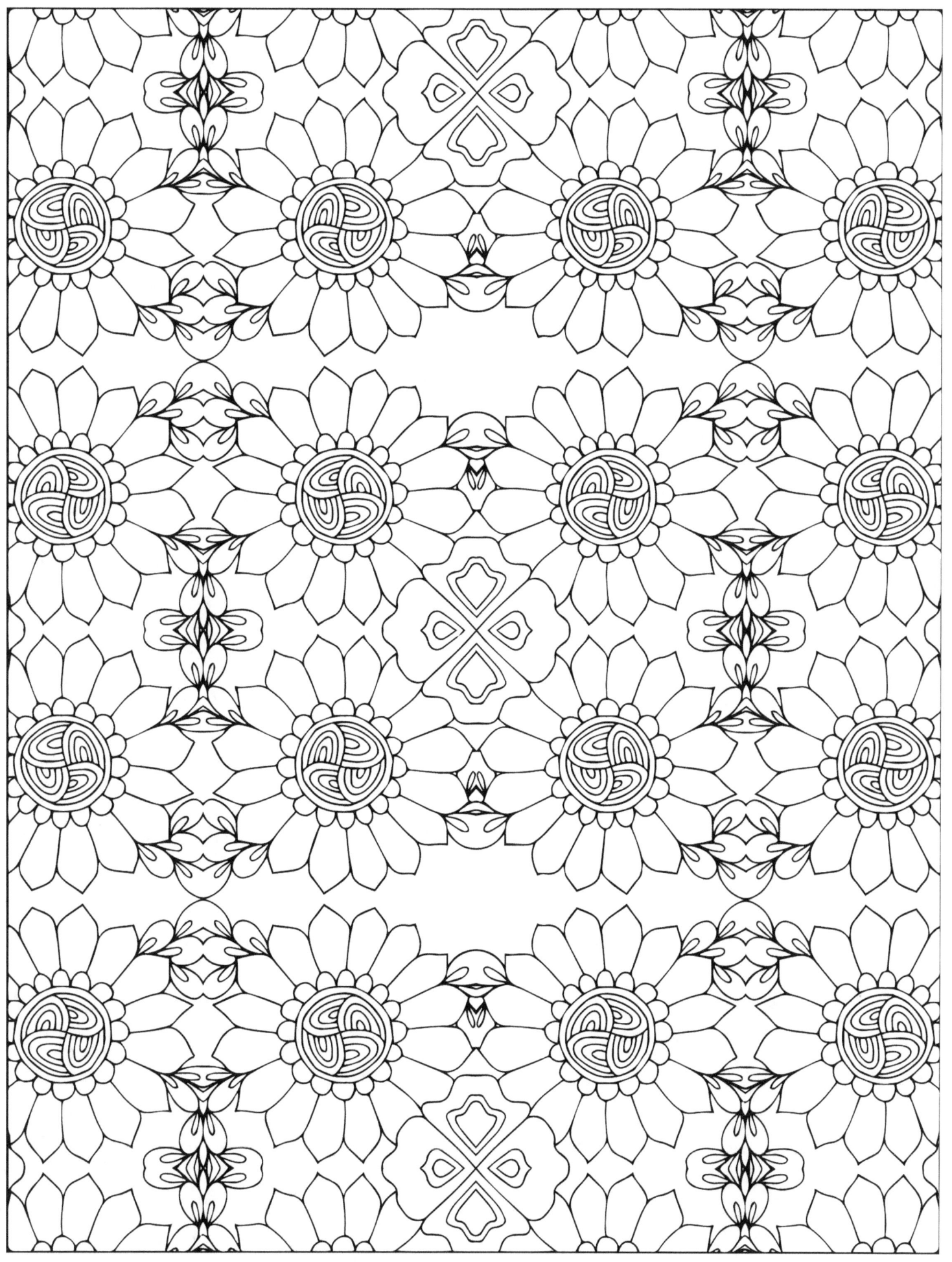

Artist: Tina Golden

Book: Fabulous Florals (Pen & Pixel Fusion Vol. 2)

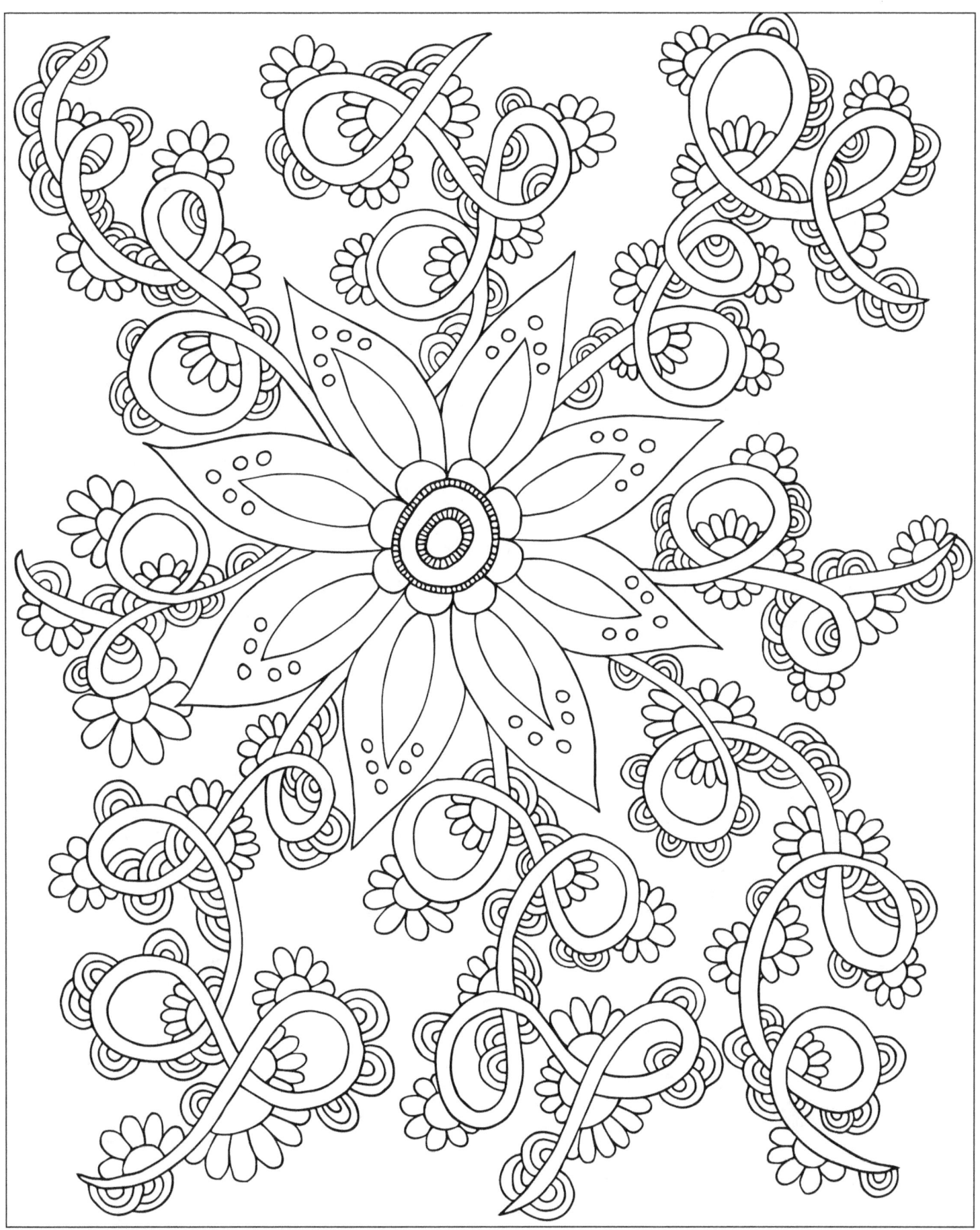

Artist: Tina Golden

Book: Fabulous Florals (Pen & Pixel Fusion Vol. 2)

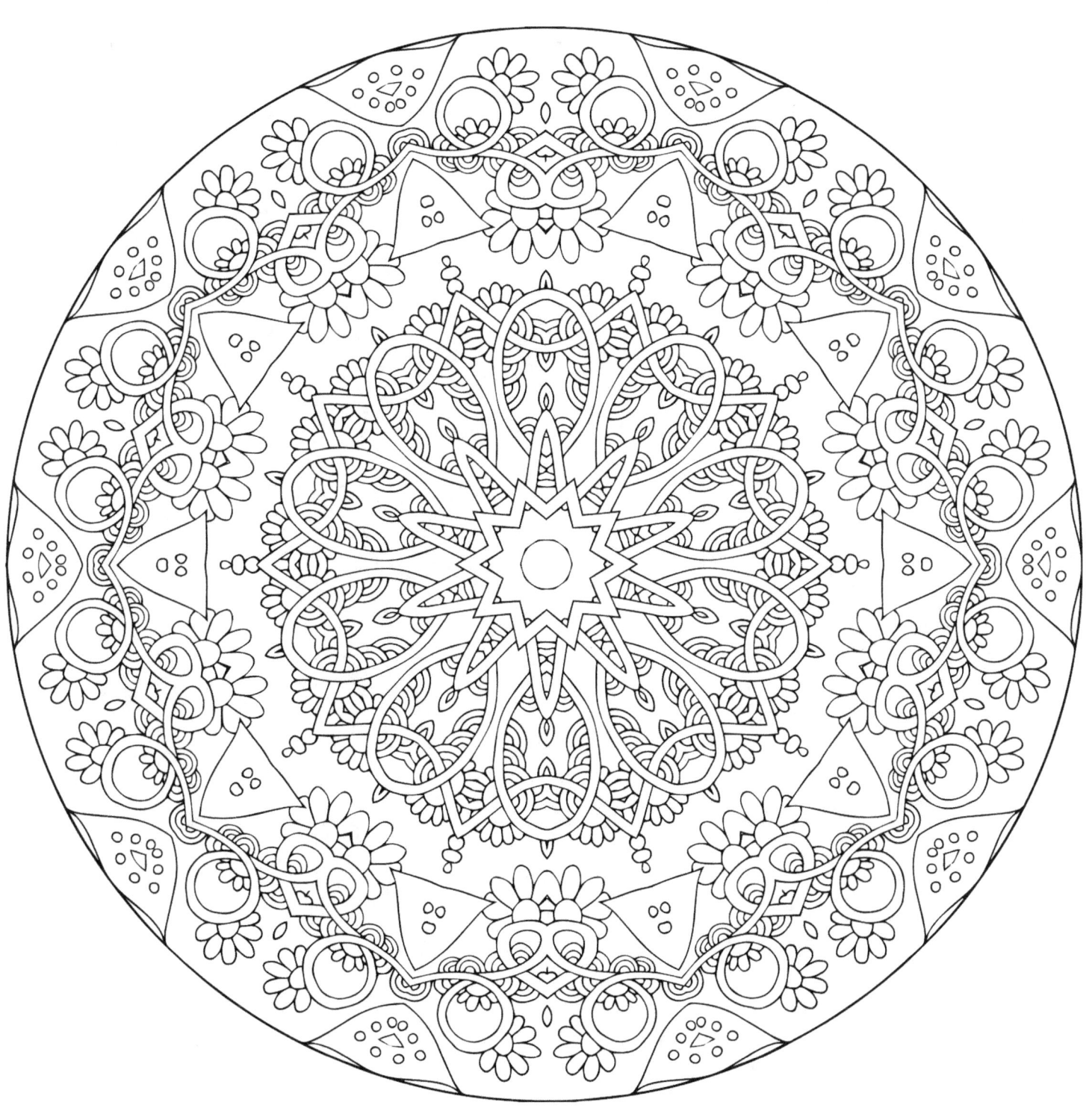

Artist: Tina Golden

Book: Fabulous Florals (Pen & Pixel Fusion Vol. 2)

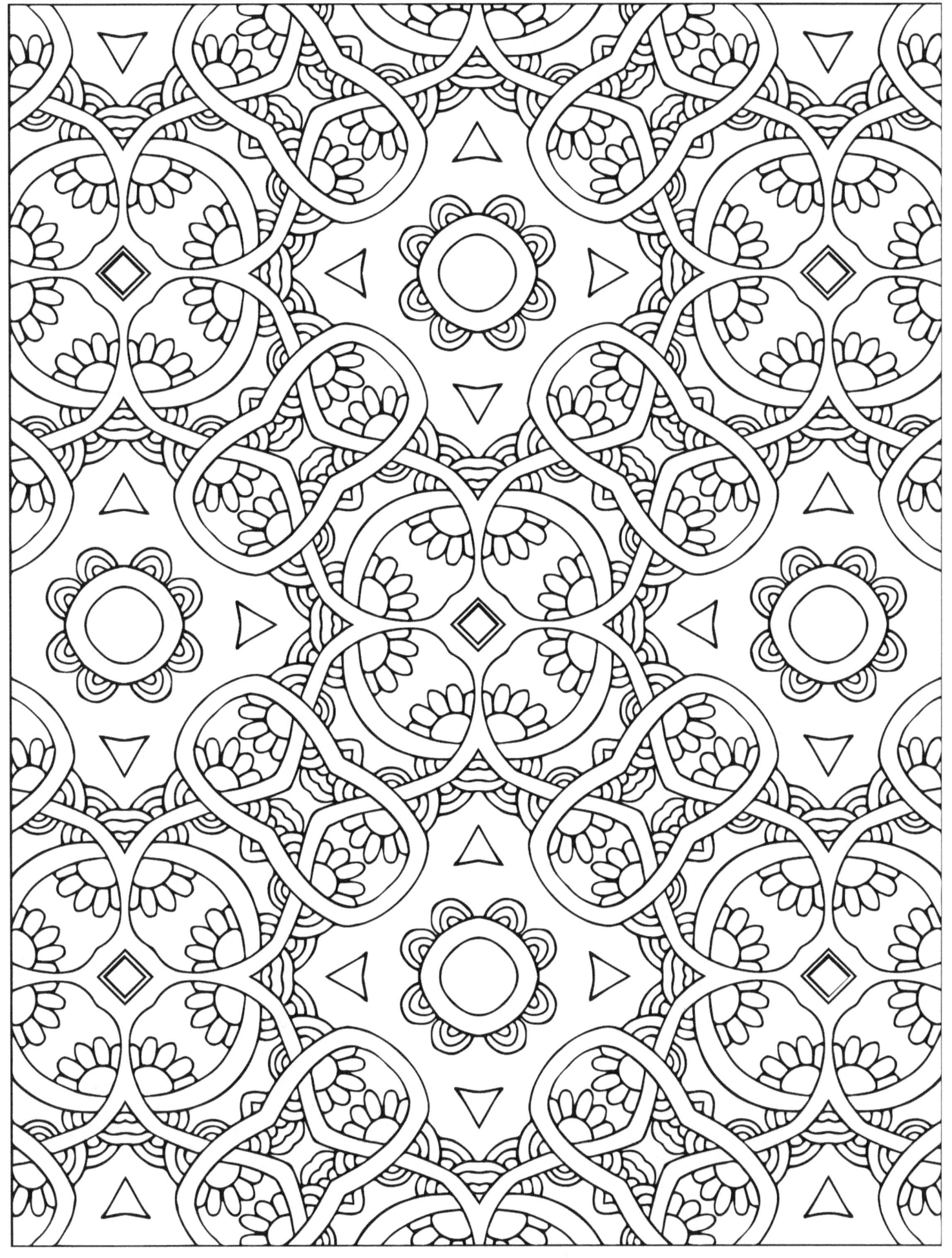

Artist: Tina Golden

Book: Fabulous Florals (Pen & Pixel Fusion Vol. 2)

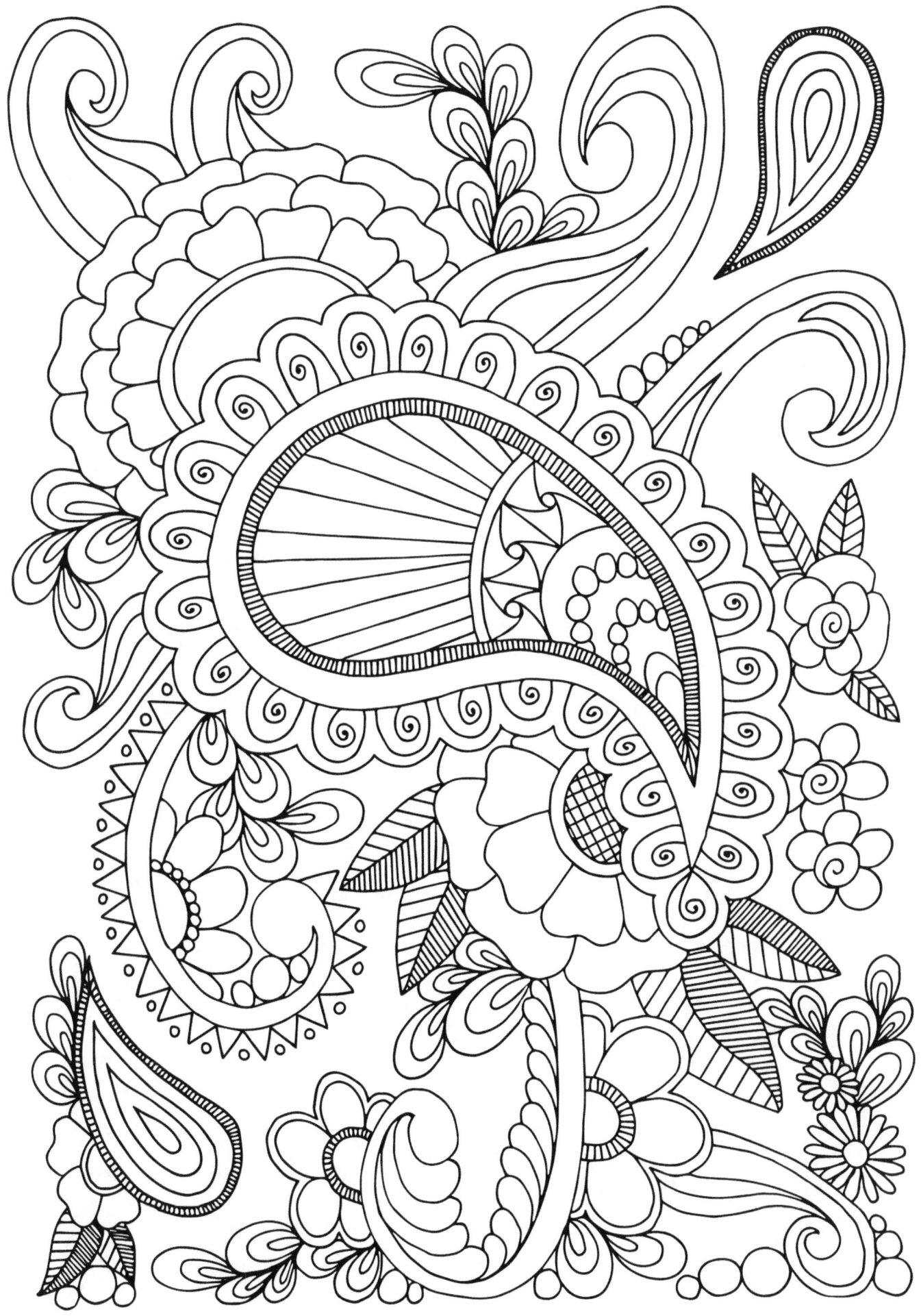

Artist: Tina Golden

Book: Fabulous Florals (Pen & Pixel Fusion Vol. 2)

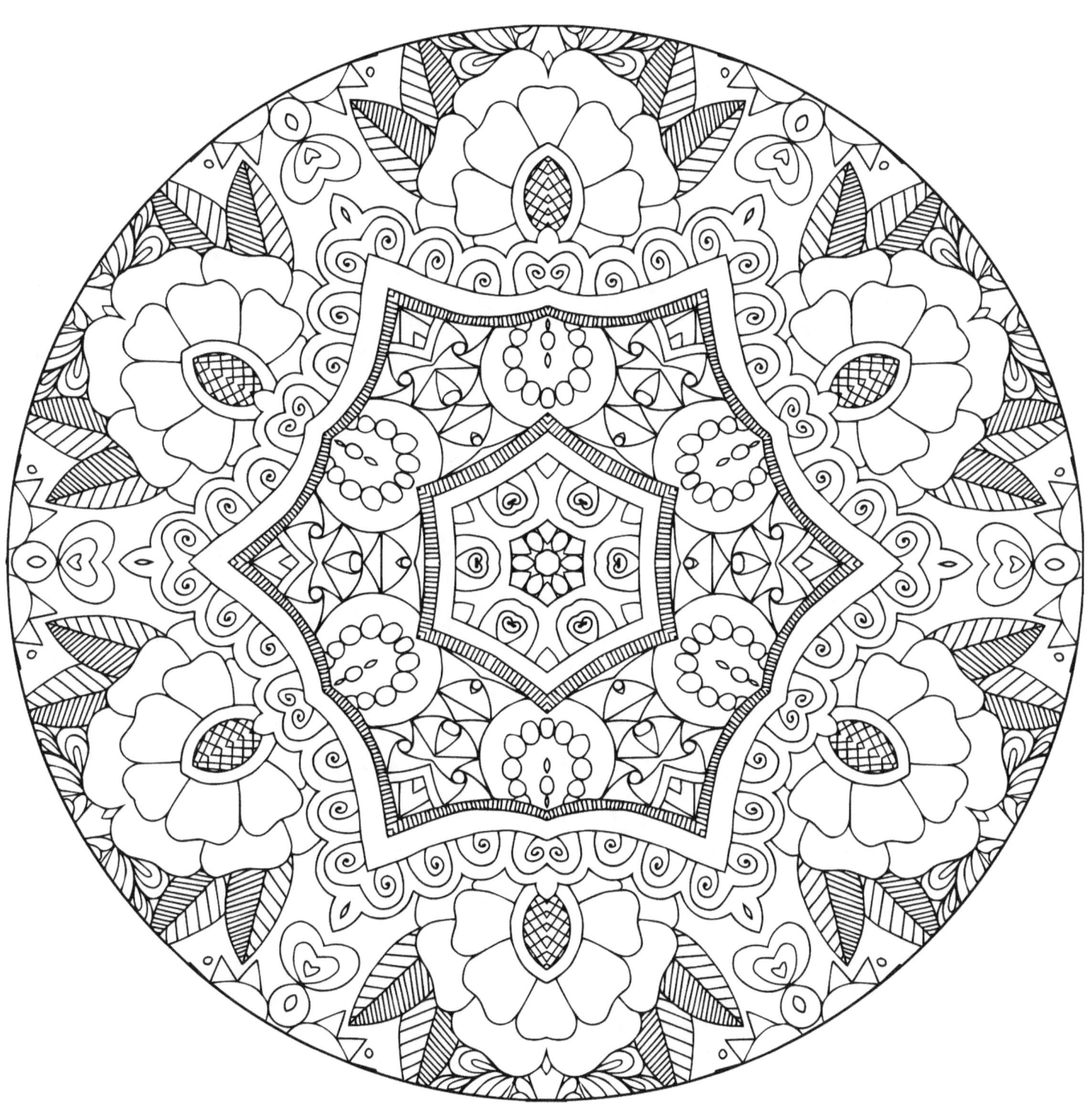

Artist: Tina Golden

Book: Fabulous Florals (Pen & Pixel Fusion Vol. 2)

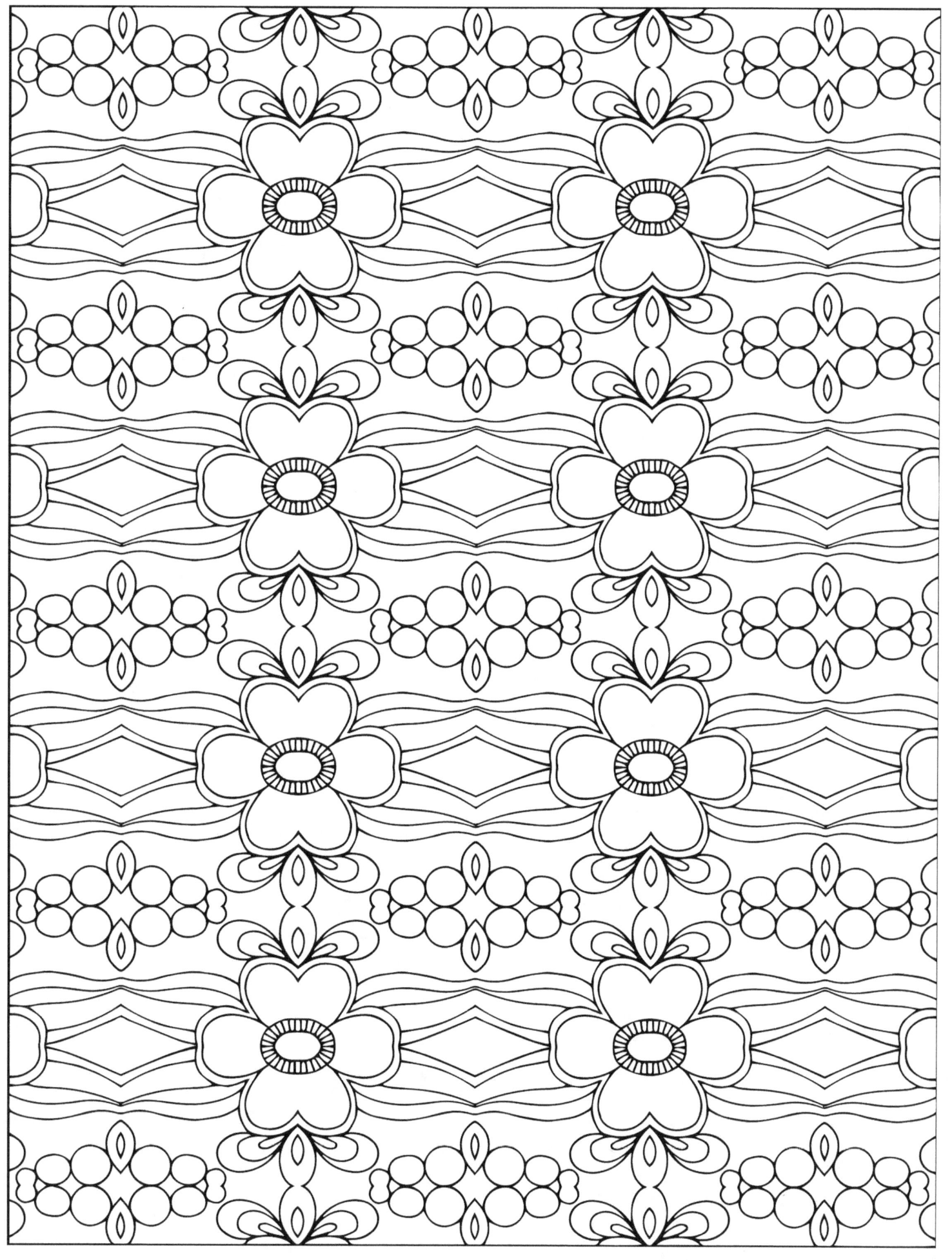

Artist: Tina Golden

Book: Fabulous Florals (Pen & Pixel Fusion Vol. 2)

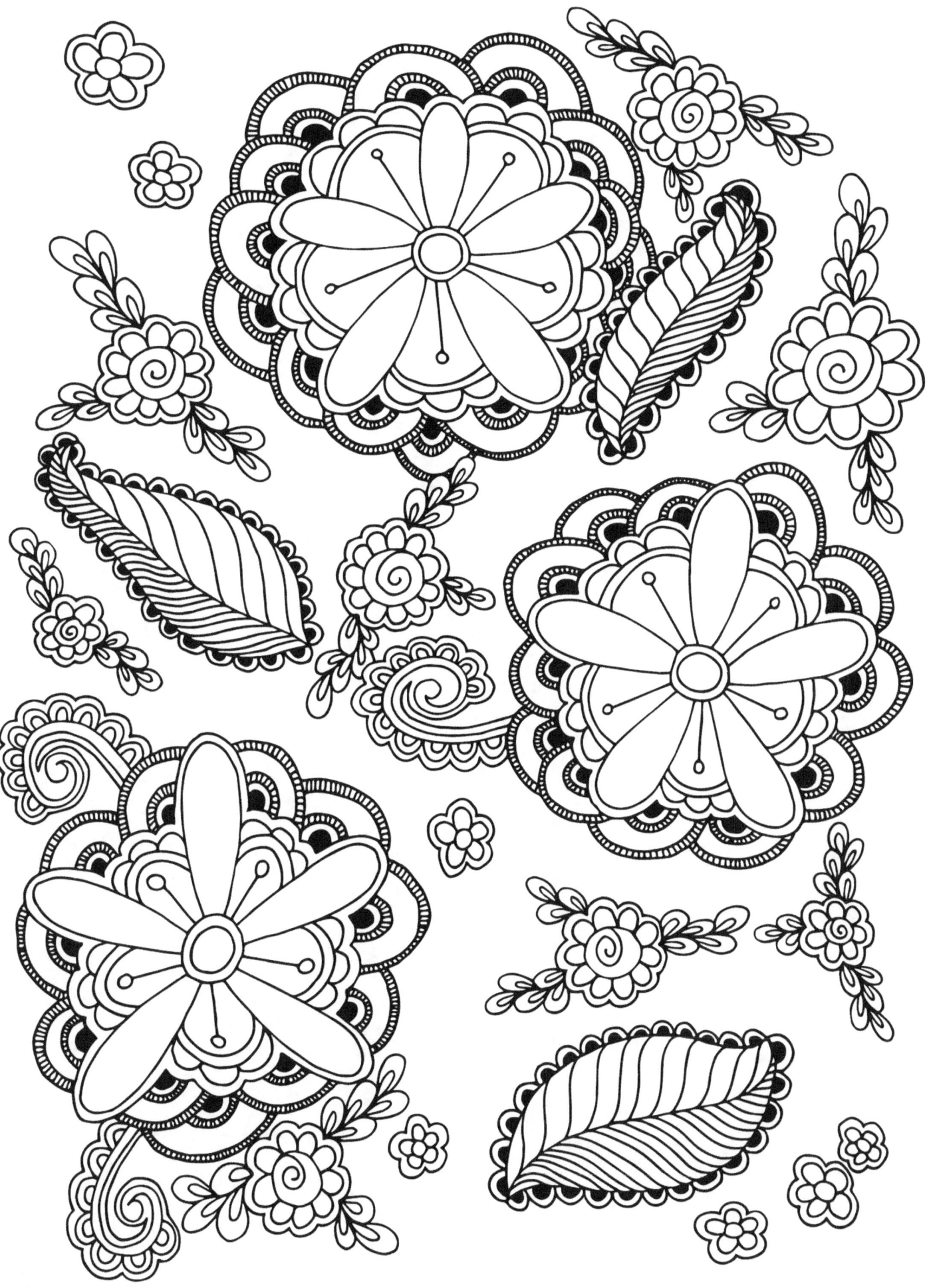

Artist: Tina Golden

Book: Fabulous Florals (Pen & Pixel Fusion Vol. 2)

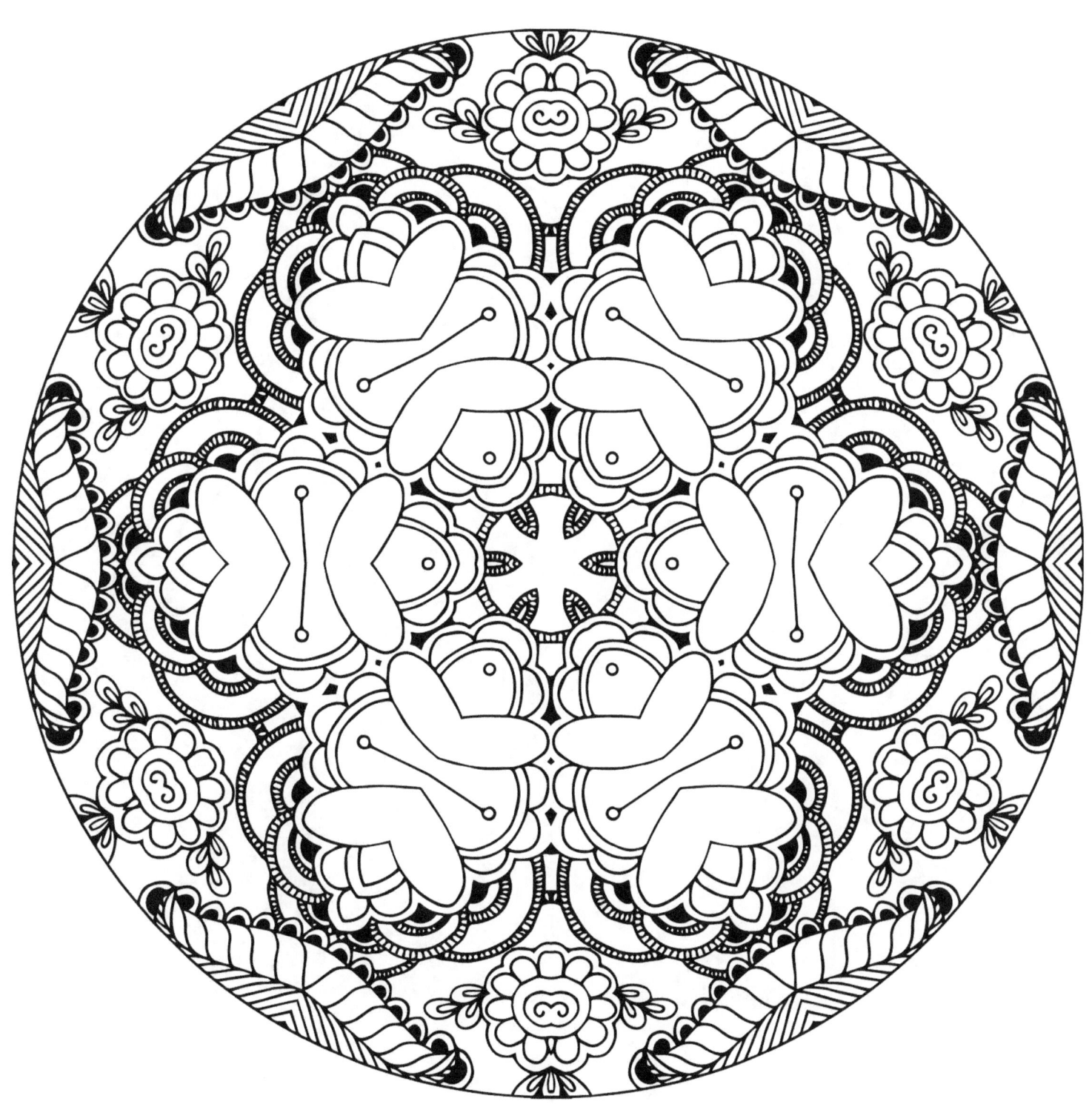

Artist: Tina Golden

Book: Fabulous Florals (Pen & Pixel Fusion Vol. 2)

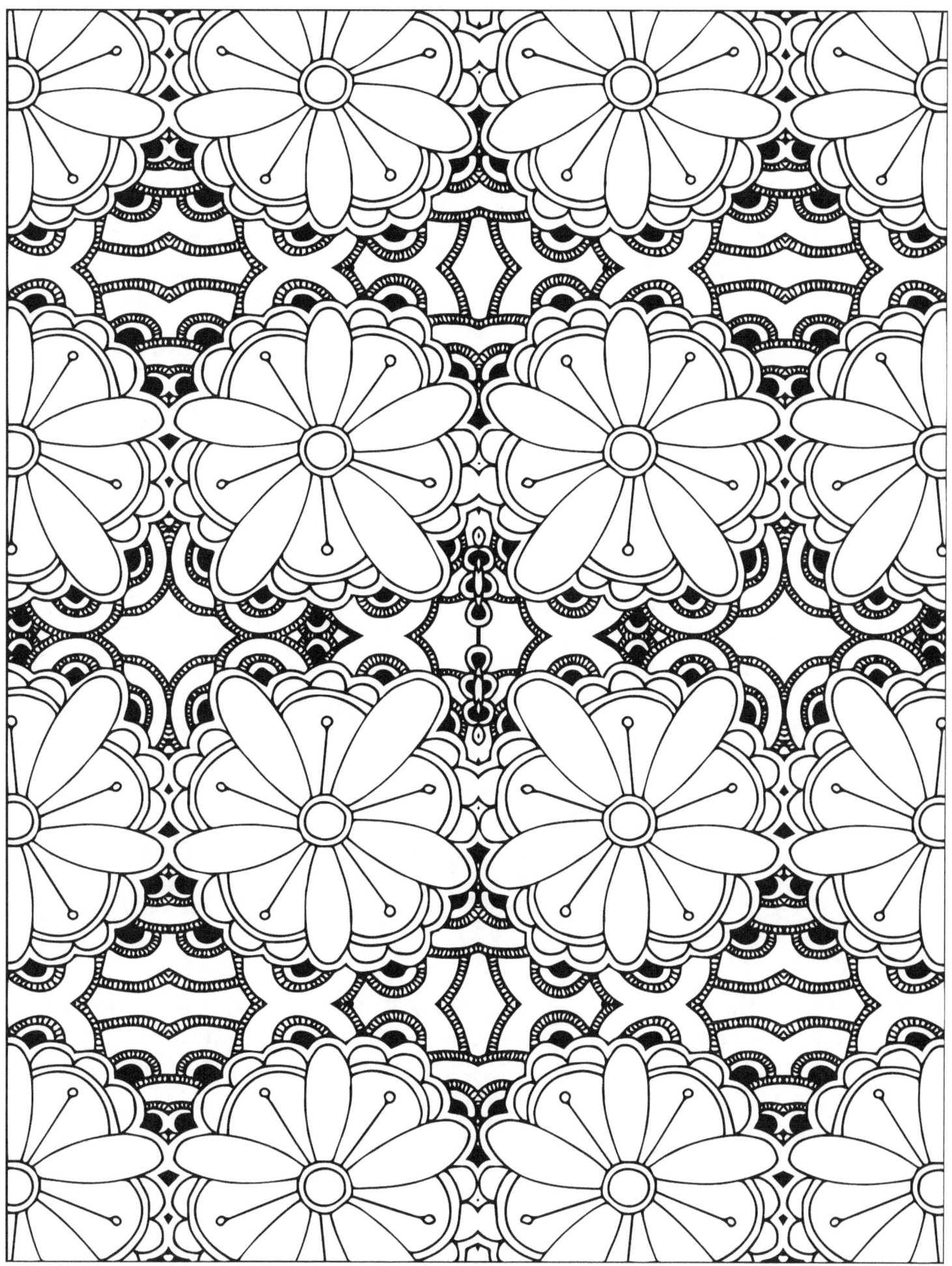

Artist: Tina Golden

Book: Fabulous Florals (Pen & Pixel Fusion Vol. 2)

Blotter Page

Remove and Insert Between
Pages if Using Wet Media

Blotter Page

Remove and Insert Between
Pages if Using Wet Media

Blotter Page

Remove and Insert Between
Pages if Using Wet Media